IN QUEST OF Big Fish

HENRY WASZCZUK AND ITALO LABIGNAN

IN QUEST OF *Big Fish*

KEY PORTER BOOKS

799.12
WAS

Copyright © 1996 by Henry Waszczuk and Italo Labignan

All rights reserved. No part of this work covered by the copyrights hereon may be reproduced or used in any form or by any means – graphic, electronic or mechanical, including photocopying, recording, taping or information storage and retrieval systems – without the prior written permission of the publisher, or, in case of photocopying or other reprographic copying, without a licence from the Canadian Reprography Collective.

Canadian Cataloguing in Publication Data

Waszczuk, Henry, 1950–
In quest of big fish

ISBN 1-55013-735-2

1. Fishing.   2. Fishes.   3. Fishing – Guidebooks.
I. Title.

SH441.W38 1995   799.1'2   C95-931626-4

Key Porter Books Limited
70 The Esplanade
Toronto, Ontario
Canada M5E 1R2

Design Concept: Peter Maher
Layout: Leah Gryfe

96 97 98 99 6 5 4 3 2 1

The quest for big fish has never failed to capture attention. Zane Grey was consumed by it, and it forced Hemingway to write *The Old Man and the Sea*. Countless others, less famous but equally driven, have found themselves drawn to the water to search for the mysteries it holds, and dedications to their passion inscribe plaques along our waterways and headstones across our continent.

In its small way, this book salutes the drive for which these men are remembered, but it salutes as well the young and the new to the sport of fishing and welcomes all to this path that has been well but lightly trodden. For each of you who has stared intently at the water's surface and has felt the strength of the mysteries below, welcome.

Regardless of whether you have come to watch a Royal Coachman defy gravity on a riffle or to feel the thrumming of a deepwater plug, we dedicate this book to you, to the great fraternity of anglers and to the legends of the past made famous by their own *quest for big fish*.

carries on the first visit to a distant angling location would break the back of a good-sized camel. But on the next trip, he or she can usually stuff everything needed into two or three small bags.

Then there are the fish. All anglers become jaded catching the same species trip after trip. But when they travel to a distant spot, they face new species and new techniques. They may even learn new ways to tackle familiar quarry back at home.

Henry Waszczuk and Italo Labignan have made a career of traveling to distant places in quest of big fish. Their travels have taken them all over the world.

If you've never made an exotic fishing trip, I urge you to do so. It will enrich your angling experiences forever, while giving you a clearer understanding of the world and all the wonderful people who live in it.

Lefty Kreh

Foreword

Fishing Distant Waters

Fishing is always exciting. Catching a large fish adds to the thrill. And traveling to a distant, exotic place and catching large fish that you can't find at home, especially one of trophy proportions, may be one of the greatest thrills in angling.

Travel also offers the opportunity to meet and observe people. In parts of the South Pacific, people live much as they did hundreds of years ago. They still hunt with bows and arrows or pointed sticks. They use dugout canoes fashioned from giant logs, perhaps with outriggers on one side to lend some stability to their narrow craft. While in New Guinea several years ago, our group met a man in a dugout canoe transporting watermelons. He offered us two of them, but with a strange request. We had to bring the seeds back. You see, since there are no stores there where he could buy watermelon seeds, the only way to continue growing melons was to plant the seeds from the ones we ate.

The boats in faraway places are also fascinating. To watch a boat plunge through whitewater rapids, or glide ghost-like over a bonefish flat, or even move upstream with grace and power reminds me of the generations it has taken to design craft ideally suited to local waters. These boats put the people's individuality in a tangible form.

In addition to the new experiences, distant angling trips provide an opportunity to try your luck on rarely fished waters. New and strange waters are always bewitching. What a difference there is between the dark, roiled jungle rivers and the incredible clarity of a New Zealand stream; between a lily-pad-covered cypress swamp in Florida and the dark, green, mysterious waters of a lake in northern Canada.

The flies, lures, and tackle vary widely when you fish in different parts of the world. The gear that the average person

Contents

Introduction

Nothing can stir the heart and soul of an angler like the quest for big fish. The delights come in all forms – from repeatedly casting to a spot where you saw a big one jump to planning a major expedition halfway around the world for trophy fish of a species you've never seen before. As they say, it's all in the chase.

But no chase is rewarding without the opportunity to catch a fish. Toward that end, Henry Waszczuk and Italo Labignan have produced the most authoritative guide to catching the trophy specimens of 35 of the world's leading freshwater and saltwater gamefish. In this book you'll find everything from the best time to go, what to bring, what to use, and even where to stay. You'll also learn what to do to bring a big fish to hook and, ultimately, to hand. It's as complete a guide as you can possibly get within a single book.

In Quest of Big Fish won't steer you to any particular place or any particular species of fish. Rather, the authors have attempted to show anglers what's out there, waiting for them in waters all over the globe. After all, it's easy to grow a little tired of catching the same fish over and over again. Anglers who live in remote parts of Canada may pine for the chance to cast the flats for bonefish. An angler living in the southern United States, on the other hand, may view those Canadian lakes as heaven on earth, wondering just how anyone could grow bored with them. It all depends on what you're used to.

Happily, with the jet age, anglers can taste the greatest angling thrills worldwide with relatively little effort and at relatively low costs. It's never been easier to cast a line to exotic, exciting fish.

So enjoy this book. Who knows? Maybe you'll find something that starts a fire within, sending you on yet another quest for a big fish.

The Quest

Fishing is one of mankind's oldest and most diverse activities. Indeed, our fascination with fish and fishing began long before the dawn of recorded history, having grown out of necessity. After all, prehistoric man needed to eat. Successful fishermen survived, others starved. There was nothing recreational about fishing. For many early people, if they didn't catch fish, they simply didn't eat.

Testimony of ancient fishing activity can be seen in the etchings throughout North America and the hieroglyphics on the walls of Egyptian tombs. These timeless images show man spearing, seining, and bludgeoning fish. Even the Bible contains many references to fishermen, including the tale of Jonah and the whale.

The advent of farming made fishing less necessary for survival. People did not stop fishing, however. Fish remain a tasty part of the cuisine of most countries, and fishing itself was pursued for its own pleasures.

The Roman scholar Aelian also wrote about fishing. Today, hundreds of years after his words were written, we can still imagine the scene:

> The natural insect is in ill repute with the fishermen, who cannot make use of it. They manage to circumvent the fish, however, by the following clever piscatorial device. They cover a hook with red wool, and upon this, they fasten two feathers of a waxy appearance which grow under a cock's wattles, they have a reed [rod] six feet long and a fishing line about the same length. They drop this lure upon the water, and the fish, being attracted by the color, becomes extremely excited, proceeds to meet it, anticipating from

its beautiful appearance a most delicious repast. But, as with extended mouth, it seizes the lure, it is held fast by the hook, and being captured, meets with a very sorry entertainment.

Without doubt, that "very sorry entertainment" refers to the inevitable whack on the head with a rock or a big stick. After all, this was hundreds of years ago. Catch-and-release was simply unheard of.

Catching fish for fun eventually became known as angling, a reference to the angle formed by the rod or pole and the line arcing off its tip. References to angling in English literature date back more than 500 years, including the treatise on "Fishing with an Angle" and Izaak Walton's famous *Compleat Angler*.

In the 19th century, angling began to develop into the modern pursuit we know today. With North America largely tamed, a growing population began to view its waters as a playground.

Today, for millions of people all over the globe, fishing represents an opportunity to enjoy the companionship of kindred spirits while interacting with nature and participating in an exciting and challenging pastime.

For the individual angler, the pursuit of fish normally begins as a stage of confused discovery, when everything is new and simply catching fish – any fish – provides all the reward one could hope for. Before long, the angler acquires new skills, and catching lots of fish becomes a primary focus. The size or species of fish really doesn't matter, so long as there is consistent action. This quest for quantity eventually gives way to the quest for quality, as the angler learns what constitutes an exceptional catch and what doesn't. Now catching numbers of small fish doesn't matter. The angler is on a quest – a quest for big fish.

Some people describe fishing as a sport, but in view of its roots and its evolution into a recreational enterprise, it would be far more accurate to consider it a cultural pursuit. Sports have winners and losers, direct competition, and means to measure success. None of these applies to angling.

Professional fishing tournaments may add an element of competition, but for most folks a day's fishing allows an opportunity to escape. When you fish, there are no telephones, no fax machines, no advertisements to bombard you, no one to answer to. Fish do not respond to threats, bribery, or money. To paraphrase the great Robert Traver, they aren't the least bit impressed by power or one's social stature. Before a fish, all men are indeed equal. Success comes only to those quiet enough and patient enough to learn the ways of a fish's world.

Several years ago I was driving home from work on a cool, rainy afternoon in late spring. I happened upon a narrow stone bridge that spanned a small creek. Even though the largest population center in Canada loomed on the horizon just a few miles away, this tiny finger of water still flowed pure and clean, and hordes of ever-hungry brook trout thrived in its cool, dark pools. Propped up against the cracked and crumbling bridge was a child's bicycle, its yellow paint as chipped and cracked as the bridge itself.

I stopped my truck a short distance before the bridge and quietly walked along the gravel. Directly below the span was one of the deeper, darker pools on the creek, and perched precariously on a log jutting into its black water was a girl of about seven. She had a well-used length of cane, with about six feet of rather heavy line tied directly to its tip. Attached to the end of the line was a relatively large, and probably dull, hook.

I watched in silence as the young angler reached into her pocket and delicately extracted a small, wriggly earthworm. Skillfully impaling it on the hook, she then, with equal skill, swung it out into the fast water at the upstream end of the pool, allowing the current to roll it through the logs to the deepest holes where the brook trout lived. Almost immediately, her rod tip bounced, and she quickly flipped a fat little brook trout out of the water, through the air, and onto the grassy bank.

With the agility of a cat, she then leaped from her perch and tackled the trout as it flipped back toward the river. She removed the hook, admired the fish for a moment, then, to my complete surprise, slipped it gently back into the brook. It departed in an instant.

At that, the little girl turned to me (I was surprised she even knew I was there) and explained that if we don't put back the little fish, they'll never grow into big ones. "And you know," she continued, "it's the big ones that I'm really after."

I stayed and talked for half an hour while she grassed another half-dozen colorful trout, including a fish that was pushing two pounds. A two-pounder is a nice brookie anywhere, but in a brook so small that an adult could straddle it, flowing in the shadows of skyscrapers, it was a genuine monster. She let that one go, too.

That was many years ago, but I have no doubt she became a lifelong angler, and I have no doubt that since then she has caught many fish that dwarfed the best of her brook trout. But I'm equally sure that none means more to her than the orange-and-green trout from the tiny spring creek. Big fish are relative to what they are and where you find them. For that little girl, those bright little brookies were just as important as a 1,000-pound marlin.

Fishing's not a matter of greed – of wanting more and bigger – but, as the girl on the brook showed me all those years ago, it's a matter of finding ourselves. There's more to catching a big fish than simply holding it for a picture. It's a personal goal in a mass-produced, plastic-wrapped world.

May your own quest never end.

Freshwater Fish

Arctic Char

Scientific name: *Salvelinus alpinus*

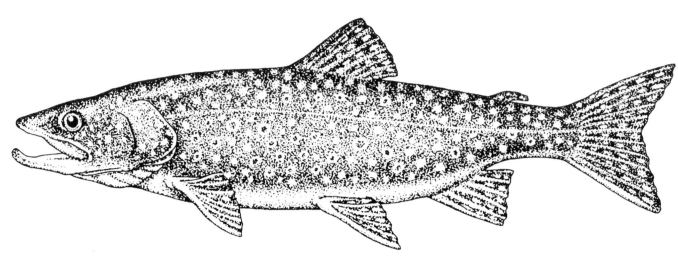

Few regions on earth are as intriguing as the Arctic – home of the Arctic char. A powerful, aggressive predator, this fish wanders icy northern waters in large schools, reaching sizes capable of testing heavy gear and the best angling skills.

Habitat and Behavior

Circumpolar in distribution, Arctic char are found in extreme northern Asia, Scandinavia, Greenland, and Iceland. In North America, Arctic char are confined to the northernmost reaches of Canada and Alaska. Throughout their range, both landlocked and anadromous (migratory) populations are found. Sea-run char average a little less than 10 pounds, although fish up to 20 pounds show up now and then. Landlocked char tend to run a little smaller, averaging four pounds.

Regardless of size, the Arctic char is among the slowest growing and longest living of all freshwater fish. Char have been known to live more than 40 years in captivity, and studies show that few reach true adulthood until their 20th birthday.

The Arctic char spawns in September and October, in water of about 39˚F. At that time, the fish assumes a darker overall coloration, usually with a dark green back and brilliant red belly, capped by fiery red spots peppering its flanks. The adult male, in particular, develops a brilliant red belly and sides. Some anglers believe these brightly colored spawning fish make the greatest trophies of all.

Finding the Heavyweights

If there's one thing Arctic char know how to do, it's eat. Hooking a monster is a matter of knowing where to look and of being in the right

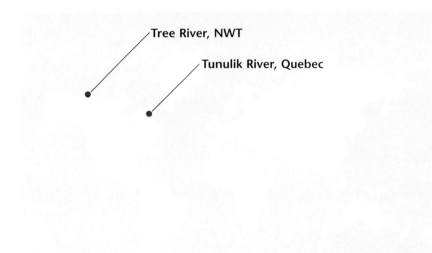

Tree River, NWT

Tunulik River, Quebec

HOT SPOTS

IGFA RECORD

ARCTIC CHAR
Weight: 14.77 kg (32 lbs. 9 oz.)
Place: Tree River, N.W.T, Canada
Date: July 30, 1981
Angler: Jeffery L. Ward

place at the right time. Anadromous char begin to lose their brilliant silvery sheen and some of their weight soon after entering fresh water, so the closer to the sea you fish, the better your chance of taking a trophy. The right time depends on latitude and location, and can range from July to mid-September.

Char travel in schools. When you find one, you will usually find others nearby. It is possible to fish numerous barren areas before finding a bonanza. This is especially true when fishing rivers, because char migrate upstream in waves.

Arctic char usually school with other fish of the same age and size. Although you may catch the odd monster swimming with younger, smaller char, it is best to look specifically for big fish. If you catch several small char in one location, it's a good bet the bulk of your catch will be composed of similarly sized fish. If you want whoppers, find a school of older fish.

Another char is landed out of the fast current waters of the Tree River, Northwest Territories.

Hooking and landing Arctic char on hardware is one thing, but with a fly rod – unbelievable!

HOT SPOT

Northwest Territories

Tree River Char Camp sits on the Tree River just seven miles upstream from the Arctic Ocean. Common sights include muskox, caribou, wolves, fox, and grizzlies.

ACCOMMODATIONS
- Main camp building
- Tent tops over wood floors

MEALS
- Full American Plan

EQUIPMENT AVAILABLE
- Boats for transportation to fishing spots

RECOMMENDED EQUIPMENT
- Light to medium spinning outfit with six- to 17-pound line
- Light to medium baitcasting outfit
- Six- to nine-weight fly outfit with both floating and sinking lines
- Heavy spoons, jigs from $1/2$- to $5/8$-ounce
- Assorted large dry and wet flies, streamers

SEASON
- July and August
- Best fishing: July and August

CONTACT
Plummer's
950 Bradford Street
Winnipeg, Manitoba
R3H 0N5

The record books don't lie: If you want a shot at a big Arctic char, Canada's far north is the place to be. Over the years, Canadian waters have produced more record-book char than all other countries combined.

Pinpointing an exact location is a bit more difficult. Arctic char thrive throughout the cold, capelin-rich waters of northern Labrador, Hudson Bay, and Hudson Strait in the east, all the way to Alaska in the far west. Despite this enormous range, however, one area stands out: the Northwest Territories. This vast area covering more than 1,350,000 square miles offers countless lakes and thousands of miles of moving water

that produce large Arctic char. Although a number of NWT waters consistently produce large Arctic char, a handful of names keep cropping up in the record books: Coppermine River, Victoria Island, Kugaryuak River, Tree River, Hadley Bay, Koluktoo Bay, and Robinson River.

Throughout the region there are fishing lodges and fly-in camps catering to char anglers. Most promote catch-and-release policies in an effort to protect this fragile resource for future generations.

Plummer's Tree River Char Camp
Home of world-record Arctic char and fly rod records, Plummer's

Fishing Techniques

Its physical beauty and delicate appearance make it easy to underestimate the power of an Arctic char. Anglers who do so are in for a surprise, especially those fishing for anadromous char, which, like salmon, spend a good portion of their life in salt water.

Although not known for long, aerobatic fights, char slug it out with long, fast, powerful runs, steamrolling across the bottom with bulldog strength. Prying a big one off the bottom can be a trick. It is nothing for char to strip fly reels well down to the backing, or test the backbone of stout spinning rods. Runs of several hundred feet are normal, and there is not much an angler can do except hold on and hope for the best. Add the force of harsh northern tides and you're in for the fight of a lifetime.

Because of their perpetual appetite and willingness to eat just about anything, char are among the easiest game-fish to catch on flies and spoons. Indeed, few fish attack artificial offerings with such abandon. Their remote habitat and low angling pressure contributes to this behavior.

But it is still important to use the right techniques. Obviously, char can't attack a lure if they can't see it. Since Arctic char, like other trout and salmon, spend most of

HOT SPOT

Quebec

Quebec's rugged Ungava region offers some of the world's finest Arctic char fishing. Although the majority of IGFA record char have so far come from the Northwest Territories, many experts feel it is only a matter of time before a Quebec fish smashes the record.

Tunulik Arctic Adventures
Tunulik Arctic Adventures operates an outstanding fishing camp on the Tunulik River, which hosts one of the Ungava region's best trophy char runs. Fishing this area demands careful attention to the tides, which rise and fall dramatically. It is the tide's powerful currents that draw silvery, fresh-run char in enormous numbers.

ACCOMMODATIONS
• Main lodge and cabins

MEALS
• Full American Plan

EQUIPMENT AVAILABLE
• Boats as transportation to fishing spots

RECOMMENDED EQUIPMENT
• Light to medium spinning outfit with six- to 17-pound-test line
• Light to medium baitcasting outfit
• Six- to nine-weight fly outfit with both floating and sinking lines
• Heavy spoons, jigs from $1/2$- to $5/8$-ounce
• Assorted large dry and wet flies, streamers

SEASON
• July and August
• Best fishing: July and August

CONTACT
Tourisme Québec
P.O. Box 979
Montreal, Quebec H3C 2W3

Arctic Adventures
19950 Clark Graham
Baie d'Urfé, Quebec H9X 3R8

medium-sized and smaller versions excel in shallow, clear conditions.

For most Arctic char fishing, medium-action baitcasting or spinning outfits with 10- to 12-pound monofilament do a splendid job, though a large fish in heavy water can prove a challenge.

Fly fishermen normally find a nine-weight salmon rod with matched sinking or sinktip line, plus plenty of backing, can handle most big char. For the ultimate test, try using a light, six-weight trout rod.

A breathtaking scene as the incoming tide brings in a fresh school of char.

their time hugging the bottom, it's more important to use lures and flies that sink quickly than to select those that duplicate baitfish down to the smallest detail. Bright fluorescent colors – hot oranges, reds, and chartreuses – and finishes with a bit of sparkle work best. Try

chrome and nickel-plated spoons, and tinsel or mylar-based flies.

Since water levels can change quickly in the far north, it pays to carry a wide selection of lures in a variety of weights. Larger, heavier offerings work better in deep, murky water, while

Atlantic Salmon

Scientific name: *Salmo salar*

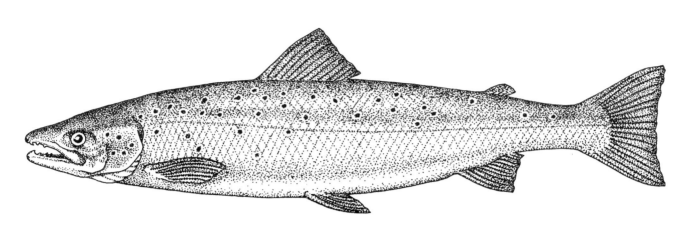

Few gamefish have achieved the notoriety of the Atlantic salmon. Anglers have revered them for hundreds of years. The fish has been called lordly, noble, and even king of gamefish.

Anglers who have never hooked one may wonder how any fish could live up to such a billing. Yet all it takes is one Atlantic salmon on the end of a line to convince any doubter that it is not just hype. Atlantic salmon truly are grand fish.

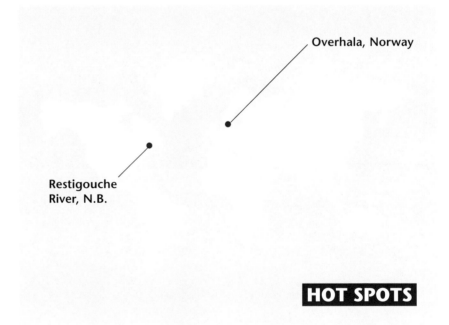

Overhala, Norway

Restigouche River, N.B.

HOT SPOTS

Habitat and Behavior

The Atlantic salmon lives only in the north Atlantic, roughly from New England north through Atlantic Canada, then east across the Arctic Circle past Greenland and Iceland to Scotland, England, and sporadically south all the way to Portugal. Norway and Sweden offer excellent salmon fishing, with many large fish.

Atlantic salmon are anadromous: They hatch in fresh water, migrate to the sea, where they grow and mature, then return to fresh water to spawn. Atlantic salmon enter spawning rivers any time from April to July. They arrive in prime condition, with bright silver sides, dark backs, and flanks peppered with distinctive black X-shaped marks. Soon after entering fresh water, both sexes become darker and may appear bronze or dark brown as spawning time approaches. The males form a striking-looking hook, known as a kype, on the lower jaw.

Finding the Heavyweights

The Atlantic salmon is among the largest fish that can be taken on a fly in fresh water. Most Atlantic salmon weigh from 12 to 30 pounds. Anything more than that is a true trophy, not only because

IGFA RECORD

ATLANTIC SALMON
Weight: 35.89 kg (79 lbs. 2 oz.)
Place: Tana River, Norway
Date: 1928
Angler: Henrik Henriksen
(representative size shown)

there are so few of them, but because they do not come readily to the fly, the only legal means of angling for them in most places.

Some rivers are famous for their runs of grilse – young, early-maturing salmon up to about six pounds.

Once native to Lake Ontario, Atlantic salmon are now being reintroduced to the Great Lakes. Historically these fish have not exceeded 30 pounds, although with more baitfish in the system today, fish could reach greater sizes.

Fishing Techniques

The exceptions, where you can fish for them with hardware or bait, include the Great Lakes and some areas in Britain and Europe. Spring fishing is usually with large, wet flies (size six or four, often tied on double hooks), heavy leaders, and sinking or sink-tip fly lines. As the season progresses and water levels recede to normal flow, smaller flies (sixes and eights) are the standard, with anglers switching to even smaller flies under warm, extreme low-water conditions. Floating lines are best during these conditions, along with leaders of eight to nine feet in six- or eight-pound test. In the broad sense, the lower and clearer the river, the smaller the fly and lighter the tackle. Later in the season, salmon may begin to take dries. Dry-fly fishing for salmon is one of

The body of the Atlantic salmon is five times longer than it is deep.

the most exciting experiences in all angling.

Hooking fish is a matter of fishing the right spots. The salmon lie (holding area) may be nothing more than a slick in the tail end of a pool, or break in the current, often in water as shallow as three to four feet.

While Atlantic salmon over 30 pounds may be uncommon, a handful of Canadian rivers are known for consistently producing big fish, among them the Matapedia, Restigouche, Moisie, and Grand Cascapedia. Many other rivers produce salmon in the 20-pound class – still highly respectable fish. Rivers of the Gaspé and north shore of the St. Lawrence in Quebec tend to produce big fish early, while New Brunswick rivers produce their biggest salmon later in the season. On rivers of northern Quebec, Newfoundland/Labrador, and Nova Scotia, the larger salmon are usually late arrivals.

With rare exceptions, all salmon return to their parent river for spawning.

HOT SPOT

Norway

Few places produce more gigantic Atlantic salmon than Norway, which is blessed with more salmon rivers than any other spot on earth. Many produce huge salmon, including the world's largest. Not surprisingly, visiting anglers must pay a heavy premium to try their luck.

Since many of Norway's salmon rivers are turbulent and not well suited to flyfishing, plugs and spoons are popular with local anglers. However, some rivers offer a good chance at catching truly huge fish on the fly. The sturdy, two-handed fly rods used by many Norwegian anglers are well suited to fishing for big salmon in turbulent waters. The heavy flow also makes your choice of a leader important. Better to go a touch too heavy than risk snapping off a trophy.

Local flies are preferred by guides, but hair-wing and feather-wing patterns used on Canadian rivers are also effective. In heavy water, size 1/0 to 4/0 (and larger) flies are popular. Sizes two, four, and six are better in low water.

Overhala Hotel

The Overhala Hotel in Overhala, Norway, is no stranger to big fish. Early in the season, most fishing on the two nearby rivers is by boat. Later, when the water drops, bank fishing becomes productive.

ACCOMMODATIONS
• 64-suite hotel

MEALS
• All meals available in the hotel

RECOMMENDED EQUIPMENT
• Medium-heavy spinning outfit
• Medium-heavy baitcasting outfit
• Eight- or nine-weight fly outfit
• Selection of in-line spinners from size one to five
• Selection of small crankbaits
• Selection of small spoons
• Selection of wet salmon and steelhead flies: Blue Charm, Green
• Highlander, Skyomish Sunrise, Sockeye John

SEASON
• May to late August
• Best fishing: June and July

CONTACT
Norwegian National Tourist Office
655 3rd Avenue
New York, New York
10022

HOT SPOT

Restigouche River, New Brunswick

Of the major Atlantic salmon rivers in North America, the Restigouche and its tributaries are the best known for big fish. Once the run is on, which traditionally begins in early June with huge females, good fishing lasts to the end of the season. Prime time most years is from about mid-June through mid-July. The average Restigouche salmon is about 20 pounds, with a reasonable chance of hooking one up to 35 or 40 pounds.

The water is apt to be high during this period, so sinking or sink-tip lines and large flies are the norm. Once water levels recede by mid-July, huge fish are still possible, but grilse and first-time spawners running up to 20 pounds make up the bulk of the catch. Weight-forward floating lines and leaders from eight- to 12-pound-test take over during the second half of the season. Flies such as the Rusty Rat, Silver Rat, Black Rat, Green Highlander, Silver Doctor, Black Dose, Jock Scott, Lady Amherst, Muddler and Blue Charm, in sizes from four to eight, are all good. Should you wish to try fishing dries later on, go with the Brown Bomber, Bivisible, Royal and White Wulffs, and MacIntosh in size eight and 10. Nearly all fishing on the Restigouche is done from boats, except in some upstream areas.

Much of the Restigouche is controlled by clubs and other private holdings. Some water in downstream sections is controlled by the Quebec government (and subject to a daily fee), and small pockets of upstream water are owned by New Brunswick. But because demand is great, the daily fees are quite high. The best bet for anglers interested in trying the mighty Restigouche is to contact the New Brunswick or the Quebec tourism departments.

New Brunswick Tourism
P.O. Box 12345
Fredericton, New Brunswick
E3B 5C3

Tourisme Québec
P.O. Box 979
Montreal, Quebec
H3C 2W3

The Atlantic salmon is a highly prized game and food fish.

The classic method of taking Atlantics is with a fly rod.

Brook Trout

Scientific name: Salvelinus fontinalis

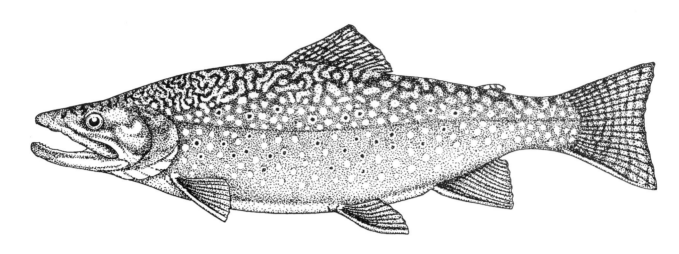

Brook trout, which eagerly consume even the most crudely impaled worms on the sloppiest of presentations, have made countless boys and girls into life-long anglers. Brookies also rank as the prettiest trout, and arguably the prettiest fish in fresh water. No other freshwater fish in North America can hope to match its crimson red belly, emerald sides, and forest green back. As are other members of the char family, they are characterized by light spots over a dark background (true trout have dark spots over a lighter body).

Habitat and Behavior

Originally brook trout were found exclusively in the eastern regions of North America, from Hudson Bay east to Labrador, and south as far as Georgia. Today you can find scattered pockets of them across Canada and the United Sates. Brook trout have even been introduced in

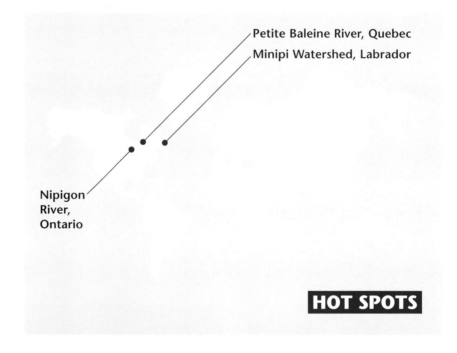

Petite Baleine River, Quebec

Minipi Watershed, Labrador

Nipigon River, Ontario

HOT SPOTS

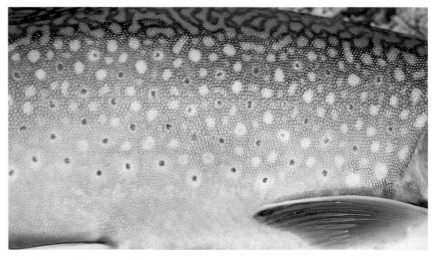

This beautiful gamefish is distinguished by red spots with blue aureoles on the sides.

New Zealand and Argentina. The best fishing, however, continues to be in eastern Canada, specifically Quebec and Labrador. Throughout most of their range, they average one pound, although brookies in remote lakes can grow considerably larger. They spawn in late summer or early fall, depending upon latitude. Truly a fish of cold waters, brookies prefer water below 68˚F.

Brook trout are carnivorous, even opportunistic, when it comes to filling their stomachs and, for that reason, have a reputation as an easy catch. But few fish are as in tune with their environment as brook trout. They can spook very quickly, and it pays to employ a cautious approach at all times.

Finding the Heavyweights

The world-record brook trout is a 14½-pounder caught in Ontario's Nipigon River in 1916. Although anglers have caught brook trout up to 11 pounds in recent years, this mark will probably never be surpassed. Reports of a 13-

IGFA RECORD

BROOK TROUT
Weight: 6.57 kg (14 lbs.8 oz.)
Place: Nipigon River, Ontario, Canada
Date: July 1916
Angler: Dr. W. J. Cook
(replica shown)

This nine-and-a-half-pounder was caught by trolling a Rapala shad rap.

HOT SPOT

Petite Baleine River, Quebec

In the tundra of Quebec's far north, south of Ungava Bay, drains the Caniapiscau River. A major tributary, the Petite Baleine River, is legendary for speckled trout in the three- to eight-pound class. The Caniapiscau provides the angler with the classic land-locked salmon, the ouananiche, as well as trophy lake trout.

Explo-Sylva Outfitters
Explo-Sylva Outfitters has been organizing fishing trips in the far north for over 15 years. Packages include housekeeping plan accommodation, or American Plan for more comfortable accommodations in the main lodge, with modern conveniences, great hospitality, and food in wilderness surroundings.

ACCOMMODATIONS
• Main lodge with all facilities, or housekeeping accommodation
• Seven-day packages available

MEALS
• American Plan or housekeeping facilities

EQUIPMENT AVAILABLE
• Boat with outboard motor and unlimited gas for three persons

SEASON
• August 10 to September 30

• Best trophy fishing before September 7

RECOMMENDED EQUIPMENT
• Medium-light spinning outfit with four- to eight-pound test, or a six- to eight-weight fly outfit with four- to eight-pound tippet
• Baitfish-imitating spoons, spinners, crankbaits and jigs up to ½ ounce (ideal in heavy currents), and/or assorted streamer flies such as the Muddler Minnow, Mickey Finn or Spuddler, plus assorted dry flies in sizes 10 and 12.

SEASON
• June 1 to September 10
• Best trophy fishing: June to early July, and early August to mid-September

CONTACT
Tourisme Québec
P.O. Box 979
Montreal, Quebec H3C 2W3

Explo-Sylva (Outfitter)
P.O. Box 4902
Succursale Place Versailles
Montreal, Quebec
H1N 3T6

---

pound brook trout, also from the Nipigon, caused a considerable stir in the late 1980s, but the fish was found to be a splake – a brook trout/lake trout hybrid.

Any brookie over five pounds is a genuine trophy, and the best locations to bag a bruiser are the remote northern lakes of Quebec and Labrador. In some locations you can also catch sea-run brook trout (called coasters), which reach impressive sizes.

Since brook trout are most active in water from 55˚F to 60˚F, the best fishing in the north is in July or August.

Fishing Techniques

Heavyweight brook trout are real meat eaters. For that reason, streamers and bucktails, along with fish-imitating lures and plugs, generally produce the most trophies. Minuscule flies are not the answer.

Brook trout are strong fish, but normally quite manageable on light- to medium-weight gear. For this reason, light- to medium-action rods and reels usually prove sufficient, even in heavy currents. Big brook trout may take out line, but a steady pressure usually brings in the fish.

Brook trout are not always found in the deepest water. In fact, some of the biggest trout, especially in remote waters, are taken extremely close to shore, often right at your feet.

Fishing is done mostly by wading in shallow water or from the shore. Boats are used to work the lakes and to reach various spots along the river. Chest waders equipped with felt soles are recommended.

Various mayflies and caddis species emerge in the area in early July and continue well into August, providing the opportunity to take huge native brook trout on dry flies. There are many thrills in the angling world, but few compare with the sight of a large brook trout rising and the subsequent disappearance of a fly in a swish of dark, peat-stained water. Streamers, bucktails and nymphs also work well.

These aren't monsters, but they are quality fish and will be great for shore lunch.

HOT SPOT

Minipi Watershed, Labrador

On the world-famous Minipi watershed, located southwest of Goose Bay, Labrador, brook trout of four to six pounds are common. Many of the lodges along this system have camp rules restricting angling to flyfishing only. Most also have bag limits of one trophy fish per guest per visit.

Minipi Lodge
Minipi Lodge, one of three lodges owned and operated by Minipi Camps, is surrounded by wilderness and some of the world's finest brook trout waters. Despite its remote location and accessibility only by helicopter from Goose Bay, the lodge is equipped with hot and cold running water, showers, electricity, and good fridges.

ACCOMMODATIONS
• Main lodge (12-person capacity)
• Minimum stay of seven days (shorter trips by special arrangement)

MEALS
• Full American Plan
• Packed shore lunches available
• BYOB

EQUIPMENT AVAILABLE
• Boats and canoes equipped with outboards

RECOMMENDED EQUIPMENT –
FLYFISHING ONLY
• Light- to medium-weight fly rods/reels (eight to nine feet for size six, seven or eight line)
• Floating and sinking or sink-tip lines, in double taper or weight-forward taper
• Leaders in four- to six-pound-test range

• Streamers: Mickey Finn, Hornberg, Black Nose Dace, Muddler (and various imitations with marabou wings in yellow, red, white, and black) in sizes four-10
• Dry Flies: Gray Fox, Henryville Special, Humpy, Adams, Irresistible, Gray Wulff, Light Cahill in sizes 10-16
• Nymphs: Atherton Dark/Medium, Badger Nymph, Montana Nymph, Hare's Ear, Isonychia Nymph, Golden Stone sizes eight-10. Other patterns are also productive
• Inquire about additional patterns when booking trip

SEASON
• June to September
• Best trophy fishing: July to August, although the potential of taking big brook trout is good throughout the season

CONTACT
Cooper's Minipi Camps
P.O. Box 340 Station B
Happy Valley, Labrador   A0P 1E0

Brown Trout

Scientific name: *Salmo trutta*

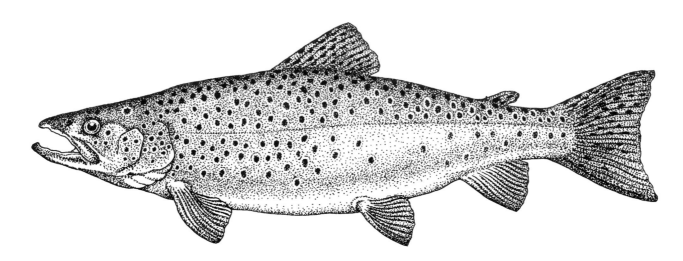

Originally confined to continental Europe and the British Isles, brown trout have been introduced into lakes and streams around the world. Today, anglers in quest of big fish can enjoy outstanding brown-trout fishing in Europe, Great Britain, North America, South America (particularly Chile), Australia, and New Zealand. There are few cold, clear streams on earth that don't hold good brown trout.

Historically, brown trout epitomized flyfishing. Almost all the old English flyfishing classics, including the treatise on "Fishing with an Angle," published in 1496, and Walton's *Compleat Angler*, from 1653, refer to the challenge of hooking the "spotted brown trout."

Habitat and Behavior

In rivers and small lakes, brown trout typically have dark chocolate brown to olive backs, butter yellow sides

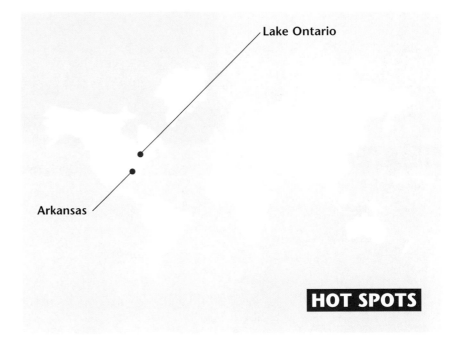

Lake Ontario

Arkansas

HOT SPOTS

covered with distinct black (and sometimes red) spots – often with bluish haloes – and creamy white bellies. Their broad tails are normally yellowish and unspotted. Large males frequently develop disproportionately large heads with severely hooked jaws, not unlike those of spent male Atlantic salmon.

Brown trout living in large lakes, or anadromous browns that migrate to the ocean, rarely develop the rich col-

oration of their stream-dwelling relatives, except for a brief spell in the fall when they spawn. Most anadromous browns resemble thick-bodied Atlantic salmon, with black backs, silvery sides, and black spots along the sides and on the gill covers. Understandably, it is quite easy to mistake the two species. However, big-water browns seldom develop the classic X-shaped spots of the Atlantic salmon. Further,

IGFA RECORD

BROWN TROUT
Weight: 18.25 kg (40 lbs. 4 oz.)
Place: Little Red River, Heber Springs,
Arkansas, U.S.A.
Date: May 9, 1992
Angler: Howard L. (Rip) Collins

while you can easily "tail" an Atlantic salmon, the stubby tail of the brown trout makes landing fish this way difficult. Browns also have broad, squared tongues, whereas the tongue of the Atlantic salmon is noticeably narrow and pointed.

Brown trout are fierce predators famed for attacking large and unusual baits. Large minnows are the preferred bait of dedicated brown-trout anglers, and many trophy browns have been caught on live mice, rigged on a small harness and fished on salmon-weight gear. Big browns that live in large streams are loners, fiercely defending their territory from any and all intruders, including small mammals.

Finding the Heavyweights

Although brown trout can reach astonishing sizes in small creeks, anadromous brown trout are the only ones that reach maximum size. Big browns – fish of 10 pounds or better – need an awful lot of food, preferably medium to large baitfish.

Since the early 1970s, the Great Lakes have produced more monster brown trout

This awesome catch tipped the scales at just over 34 pounds.

HOT SPOT

Arkansas

Although better known for its out-standing bass and crappie fishing, Arkansas has also produced a number of record-book brown trout.

RIVER RANCH RESORT
Situated just eight miles from the spot on the Little Red River where the current world-record brown trout was caught, River Ranch Resort specializes in catering to visiting anglers.

ACCOMMODATIONS
• 16-room motel
• 11 two-bedroom cabins
• Four one-room units with full kitchen

MEALS
• Available at the adjoining Chuckwagon Restaurant

RECOMMENDED EQUIPMENT
• Light to medium spinning outfit with six- to 10-pound-test line
• Nine- to 10-foot steelhead-type drifting rod
• Six- to eight-weight fly outfit with floating and sinking lines
• Selection of in-line spinners from size 0 to 4
• Selection of small crankbaits
• Selection of small jigs, particularly chartreuse twist-tail grubs

SEASON
• Best fishing: summer

CONTACT:
River Ranch Resort
630 River Ranch Road
Beaver Springs, Arkansas 72543

Arkansas Tourism
1 Capitol Mall
Little Rock, Arkansas
72201-0104

hand. Tales abound of big browns refusing all offerings while continuing to feed with abandon on real insects. Indeed, browns will refuse flies as tiny as minuscule number 24s if they don't look right.

Fishing for large browns in streams is usually a night game, using heavy gear and a large live bait. Because the best browns live near current obstructions, the fish must be hooked and landed as quickly as possible. The longer the fight, the greater chance of the trout wrapping the angler's line around a log and snapping it off.

Catching browns in big water, or migratory fish in the lower section of spawning rivers, is a different game. The angler must appeal to the fish's greed, tempting it to stuff down just one last meal before fall spawning. To be truly tempting, that last meal should be a silvery spoon, minnow plug, or even a carefully rigged baitfish.

This trophy was caught on a fly at the mouth of the Ganaraska River, Lake Ontario.

than any other area. Numerous fish have topped 30 pounds and a handful have pushed 40. Dozens of 20-pounders are landed each year. A 10-pound brown trout won't impress anyone in this area.

Large impoundments in the southern and western U.S., such as the famed Pend Oreille system, also produce big brown trout, but the Great Lakes yield more trophies.

Argentina's Rio Grande and the clear streams of New Zealand regularly produce mammoth brown trout.

Fishing Techniques

Browns are the most challenging member of the trout family, and big ones may well rank among the toughest of all gamefish to bring to

HOT SPOT

Lake Ontario

Situated in the middle of a major population area, Lake Ontario offers visiting anglers every level of accommodation and service. A fleet of several hundred charter boats serve anglers looking for browns, and in spring and fall, massive browns can be caught right off the shoreline.

Accommodations and restaurants are available in most lakeshore towns and cities. Charter boats are available on both the American and Canadian shores of Lake Ontario.

RECOMMENDED EQUIPMENT
• Long, medium-light spinning outfits with six-to 10-pound-test line for shore casting
• Downrigger-type rod and high-capacity level-wind reel for trolling
• Assortment of heavy casting spoons, such as $^1/_2$- to $^7/_8$-ounce Little Cleo, Pixie, Crocodile, Cyclops.
• Assortment of large in-line spinners up to size five
• Assortment of diving crankbaits, such as Shad Rap, Kwikfish, Lazy Ike, Tadpolly, Hot Shot

SEASON
• Year-round in Lake Ontario and the lower stretches of most tributary rivers
• Best fishing: September to January

Like most male trout, this fish has a pronounced kype.

Channel Catfish

Scientific name: *Ictalurus punctatus*

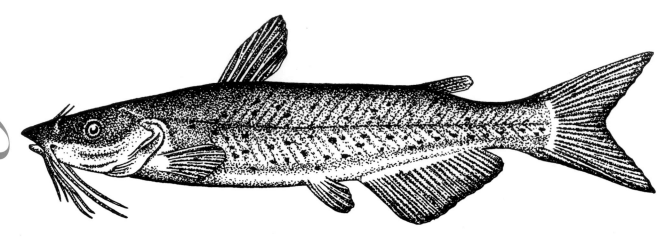

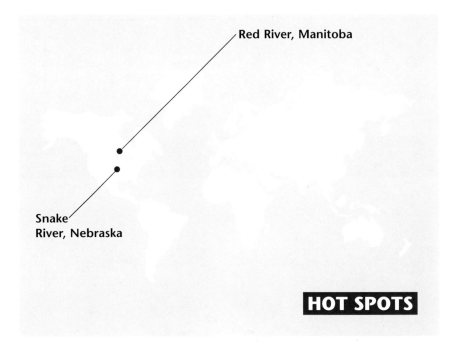

Red River, Manitoba

Snake River, Nebraska

HOT SPOTS

Although a small number of anglers have been quietly enjoying the considerable charms of this unique species for decades (particularly in the southern U.S.), it has only recently gained an international popularity. Such catfish spots as the Mississippi River, Nebraska's Snake River, and Canada's Red River, along with many reservoirs in the southern U.S., now draw anglers from around the world. Indeed, the once-lowly catfish has become a prime target of big-game anglers. That's no surprise to "cat" addicts, who point out that any fish that reaches weights of more than 30 pounds and lives in river currents and eddies powerful enough to suck down a boat has to be a formidable adversary.

The channel cat is by no means the largest member of the catfish family. In North America, both the blue and flathead catfish easily top it. The channel cat's appeal lies in its broad range, which makes it accessible to millions of eager anglers, and its reputation as an aggressive predator that will attack both bait and lures with abandon. It also tends to reach its maximum size in some of the most intimidating water anywhere, particularly the powerful tailraces below major dams – quite a contrast to the quiet bayous preferred by other members of its family. Finally, its succulent, flaky meat speaks for itself. Little wonder that the channel catfish is a favorite among anglers and restaurant patrons across North America. If you ever have a chance to order blackened catfish, do so. You'll love it!

Channel-cat coloring varies from a ruddy brown to slate gray with silvery or pale blue flanks, often randomly covered with small black spots. Cats from small rivers and streams normally show brighter coloration than their lake- or large-river-dwelling relatives.

Habitat and Behavior

The blood-curdling tales of monster catfish that swallow live animals whole are not myths but the edge of reality. It's easy to see where these wild tales come from when you consider the sheer size attained by some channel cats. Even more legendary are stories about the baits used by catfish specialists – chunks of congealed blood or rotting chicken livers are legendary.

Finding the Heavyweights

Generations of anglers who didn't know better have viewed catfish as lethargic and weak fighters. However, even small channel cats can prove tough, particularly when hooked in fast water. Larger critters test drag systems and knot strength, while real monsters regularly break rods, fry drags, and snap heavy lines. Heavy gear is the rule when fishing for big catfish. Flipping rods or downrigger outfits with 20-pound-test line are just about right.

Some of the biggest catfish come from the furious, foaming water right below major dams. Fighting a big cat in still water is a challenge. Hooking one that decides to rush into a raging current is something else again. They try anything and everything to shake free – run, hug bottom, twist line. If your line isn't top-notch, and your drag silky smooth, you don't have much chance at landing a trophy cat.

IGFA RECORD

CHANNEL CATFISH
Weight: 26.30 kg (58 lbs.)
Place: Santee-Cooper Res., S. Carolina, U.S.A.
Date: July 7, 1964
Angler: W. B. Whaley

A catfish uses its strong sense of smell to locate food.

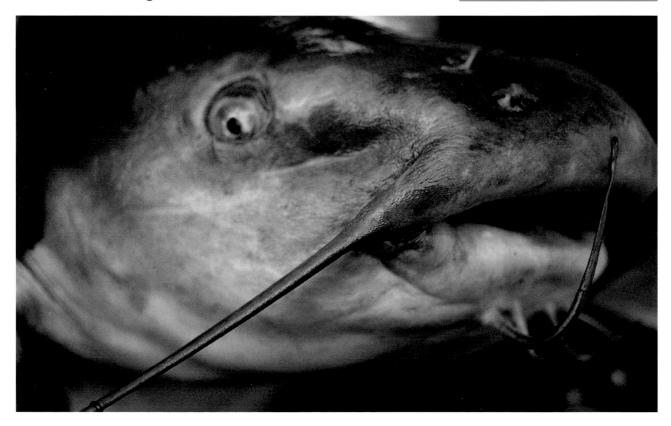

Fishing Techniques

As with other catfish, the best action for channel cats comes during low light conditions. Fishing at night, although a little eerie, is best of all. Catfish hit year-round, but are most available in the spring or early summer, when they gather in the shallows to spawn.

Channel cats can also be caught throughout the day below power dams, where surface disturbance and turbid water cut light penetration. Most shoreline anglers and boat fishermen work these areas by still-fishing with bait. Night crawlers bunched up into a ball, closely followed by large shiners or frogs, top the list of live-bait choices. Dead baits often work even better. Bait choice is largely a matter of local preference. For example, strips of goldeye work particularly well in Canada's Red River because of the abundance of this local prey. Veteran channel cat anglers everywhere use chicken liver – half-rotten ones in particular.

In backwaters off the main current, use a small hook with little weight. In heavier currents, a pyramid-shaped or large egg sinker will take the bait down. If it is drifted along the bottom with the line passing freely through the sinker, the fish can pick up the bait and run with it without feeling any resistance from the line. These finicky fish will drop bait that doesn't feel right. Once your line starts to move, drive the hook home with a quick, powerful hook set. Then hold on!

HOT SPOT

Snake River, Nebraska

The Snake River at Valentine, Nebraska, along with the Merrit Reservoir, is home to some of the largest channel cats. Accommodations are available nearby, many with full-meal packages.

Large, seaworthy walleye-style boats are advised.

RECOMMENDED EQUIPMENT
• Heavy freshwater baitcasting tackle, flipping tackle or downrigger outfits work best
• Lines from 12- to 40-pound test
• Selection of slip-sinker rigs, large forged hooks

SEASON
• Summer
• Best fishing: June

CONTACT
Tourism Nebraska
301 Centennial Mall South
Lincoln, Nebrasaka 68509

This awesome catch tipped the scales at 30 pounds.

Dams become magnets to the monster cats of the Red River in Manitoba.

HOT SPOT

Red River, Manitoba

One of the greatest channel cat fisheries in the world is on the Red River in Manitoba, Canada. Although individual fish of gigantic proportions show up in the record books from across North America, consistent trophy cats can almost always be found there. Right on its banks lies the catfish capital of the world – the town of Selkirk. So great is the city's love for channel cats that the residents erected a channel cat statue, nick-named Chuck the Catfish, in honor of legendary catfish guide, Chuck Norquay, who died on the river while doing what he loved – guiding for cats.

Although the Red River offers excellent cat fishing all summer long, the action peaks in the spring when monster cats congregate in the shallows for spawning. River holes, especially those immediately downstream from the Lockport dam – home of the 44.5-pound Canadian record – are the best spots. A variety of accommodations, some offering full-meal packages, are available in the nearby towns of Lockport and Selkirk. Restaurants of all types are also found in the immediate area.

Large, seaworthy walleye-style boats are advised.

RECOMMENDED EQUIPMENT
• Heavy freshwater baitcasting tackle, flipping tackle or downrigger outfits
• Line from 12- to 40-pound test
• Selection of slip-sinker rigs, large forged hooks

SEASON
• Summer
• Best fishing: June

CONTACT
Travel Manitoba
Department 7309
7th Floor
155 Carlton Street
Winnipeg, Manitoba
R3C 3H8

Chinook Salmon

Scientific name: *Oncorhynchus tshawytscha*

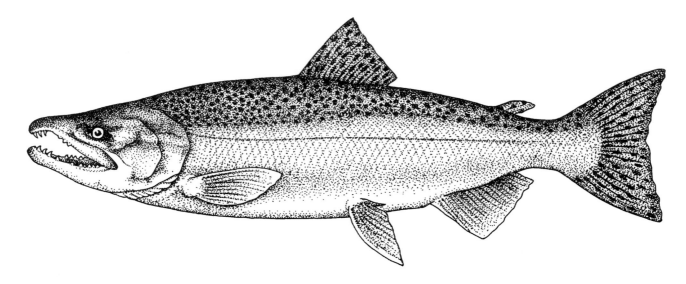

Salmon don't come any bigger than the mighty chinook, or king, salmon. These big, silvery fish average 20 to 40 pounds and have been known to top 100.

Alaskan commercial fishermen have recorded chinook salmon as large as 120 pounds. Anglers have also reported hooking fish in that size range. However, hooking a giant is one thing, and landing it is another. Big chinook rank second to none when it comes to brute strength and stamina. Trying to pry one off the bottom in 140 feet of water in a hard tide is no game for the timid.

Habitat and Behavior

Like their smaller cousin the coho salmon, chinooks have been stocked far and wide, and are now found in a number of places beyond their original home in the North Pacific. The Great Lakes hold large populations of kings, as do stocked lakes in South Dakota. New Zealand also

Kenai River, Alaska

Queen Charlotte Islands, B.C.

HOT SPOTS

has good fishing for chinooks. Although these transplanted salmon don't reach the same size as their North Pacific kin, Great Lakes kings have hauled the scales down to more than 45 pounds. Indeed, 30-pounders are just nice fish to local anglers.

Chinook salmon generally live four years, although seven-year-old salmon have been recorded. Their long life span helps them attain such incredible sizes, but kings

also get an earlier start. While coho and sockeye salmon seldom hit the big water until they're almost 18 months old, kings head for the ocean or lake within days of hatching.

Chinook wander about the big water in loose packs, following schools of smaller prey fish. Find schools of small fish and you usually find chinook. They're more light sensitive than other salmon, and often hold in deeper water, beneath the maximum level of light penetration (an area anglers like to refer to as the twilight zone). They also prefer water from 48°F to 52°F. They feed mostly when the light is low in the early morning and the evening. Night fishing can be superb, if a little eerie. As a general rule, fishing will be better on a cloudy day than on a bright sunny one.

Chinooks begin gathering near the mouths of their spawning rivers in mid to late summer. They feed heavily before making their incredible upstream voyage. Salmon often roll on the surface when they are ready to move upstream. By then most chinooks will have

IGFA RECORD
CHINOOK SALMON
Weight: 44.11 kg (97 lbs. 4 oz.)
Place: Kenai River, Alaska, U.S.A.
Date May 17, 1985
Angler: Les Anderson

darkened, their blue-purple backs and silvery sides replaced by an overall olive-brown coloration. Some Pacific fish acquire a striking red pattern that looks superficially like that of spawning sockeye. The jaws and fins of male chinooks grow to exag-

gerated proportions, and the fish begin to decay even as they move upstream.

Finding the Heavyweights

Although they're absolutely unbeatable for sheer numbers of 20- to 30-pound chinooks, the Great Lakes just don't compare to the Pacific coast for really big kings. While a whopper Great Lakes chinook might weigh from 35 to 40 pounds, Pacific fish frequently top 50 to 60 pounds every year. A 50-pound chinook is a realistic goal in many areas.

In a handful of spots, such as Alaska's Kenai River drainage, anglers target chinook over 70 pounds. Trophy kings of more than 80 pounds

Here's another monster, 81 pounds, and it was a hatchery-stocked fish . . . awesome!

HOT SPOT

Kenai River, Alaska

For almost two decades, Alaska's Kenai River has rewarded anglers seeking the very largest king salmon. While salmon stocks are declining in many Pacific watersheds, the Kenai continues to produce. As one would expect, the area has developed into a major fishing center, with all amenities available in the immediate area. For season dates and other information on fishing Kenai River kings, contact

Alaska Division of Tourism
P.O. Box 110801
Juneau, Alaska
99811-0801

Northstar Adventures

For the adventure of a lifetime in Alaska, anglers fish for trophy king (chinook) salmon on the Kenai River, and the mighty Alaskan halibut in Cook Inlet. The scenery is unsurpassed in majesty and magnitude, surrounded by lakes and streams where fishing for sockeye salmon, Dolly Varden, rainbow trout, and grayling is legendary. Your options are unlimited.

ACCOMMODATION
• European-style chalet lodge, bed and breakfast, of 16 bedrooms located on the banks of the Kenai River. Non-smoking in the lodge. Double occupancy required.

MEALS
• European-style bed and breakfast

EQUIPMENT AVAILABLE
• Licensed guides and boats
• Fly-in fishing trips
• Top-quality fishing gear

SEASON
• May to July
• Best fishing: June 15 to July 15

CONTACT
Northstar Adventures
P.O. Box 3292
Soldotna, Alaska 99669

Kenai River Sportfishing Inc.
P.O. Box 1228
Soldotna, Alaska 99669

Kenai Peninsula Tourism
11127 Frontage Road, Suite 201
Kenai, Alaska 99611

have come from this watershed, and soon somebody will finally hang one weighing more than 100 pounds.

Fishing Techniques

Fighting a big chinook is like hooking a train. It will make repeated powerful runs of up to 200 yards, and there is nothing the angler can do but hold on. Anglers frequently report being "spooled" by a chinook, the fish having run until the reel was stripped bare. Even with relatively heavy tackle, bringing a big chinook up from deep water is tough work.

Chinook are also well known for their last run. Just when the fish is at boatside and you think you have it whipped, the exhausted salmon heads for the horizon on a last desperate dash for freedom. Unprepared anglers lose many fish at this point.

Chinook differ from most other salmon in their propensity for hugging the bottom, even in open water. They're far more cover-oriented than other Pacific salmon. In the Great Lakes, anglers often catch very large chinook by dragging their lures over the bottom sand.

Trolling with spoons or darting plugs, like the J-Plug, Tomic, Lucky Louie or Lyman, is probably the best technique for catching trophy kings in big water. The key is to keep the lure well back of the boat and fish slowly. In British Columbia, oversized versions of these lures are trolled very slowly behind a rowed skiff. Smaller chinooks will chase down fast-moving plugs, but most big fish prefer slower presentations.

Perhaps the most fabled technique of all is "Hot Shotting." It involves floating down a spawning tributary, using oars or a small motor to move along more slowly than the current. Plugs (like the Hot Shot, which is so successful that the technique was named after it) are held in the current near bottom. Hot shotting is widely and successfully practiced in Pacific Coast streams and Alaska's Kenai River.

HOT SPOT

Queen Charlotte Islands, British Columbia

ACCOMMODATIONS
• A refurbished 120-foot historical paddle-wheeler
• A 10,000-square-foot steel-and-cedar lodge

MEALS
• Full American Plan
• Lounge

EQUIPMENT AVAILABLE
• Custom-built 16-foot aluminum boats with 30-hp outboards

RECOMMENDED EQUIPMENT
• 10-foot mooching outfit with 25-pound-test line
• Light spinning or baitcasting outfit with 12-pound-test line
• Buzz bombs and assorted jigging lures
• Heavy spoons for casting

SEASON
• Mid-May to mid-September
• Best fishing: May to September

CONTACT
Langara Fishing Lodge
436 West 2nd Avenue
Vancouver, British Columbia
V5Y 1E2

British Columbia has been known for its legendary salmon fishing for years, but anglers have only recently enjoyed relatively easy access to the area that many experts call the greatest salmon-fishing grounds on earth – the Queen Charlotte Islands.

Salmon from all along the Pacific Coast – from Alaska to California – gather and feed in the Queen Charlottes. The wide variety, including chinook salmon well over 70 pounds, are what fishing the Queen Charlottes is all about!

Langara Lodge
Situated at the northern tip of the Queen Charlotte Islands, Langara Lodge is in a perfect position to intercept salmon runs from a number of British Columbia river systems, including the mighty Skeena. Big chinooks are a lodge specialty. There's even a club for guests who catch fish weighing more than 70 pounds.

River-run chinooks show off brilliant color and can be taken on various lures, including a fly.

Chum Salmon

Scientific name: Oncorhynchus keta

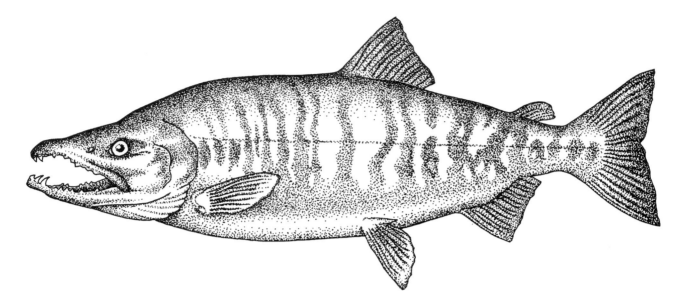

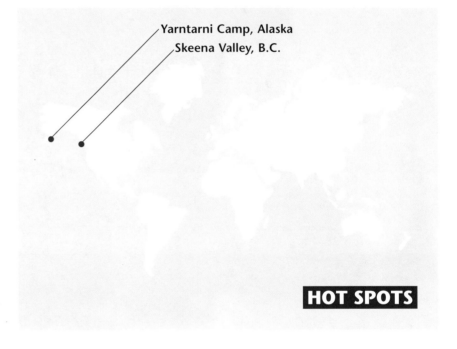

Yarntarni Camp, Alaska
Skeena Valley, B.C.

HOT SPOTS

The chum salmon's reputation as a gamefish has been overshadowed by that of the chinook and coho. However, at the right time of year and on medium to light tackle, these fish thrill anglers with fast and furious action. More than a few anglers have been left in awe upon landing a large, hook-jawed male chum with protruding teeth and a majestic purple flame pattern on its emerald flanks.

Like the smaller pink salmon, chums are heavily fished commercially, and are often sold under the name "keta salmon." With the lowest fat content of all salmon, chum are highly regarded as a food fish. Strict regulations protect the species in fresh water, leaving only a limited number of rivers in North America open to sportfishing.

Habitat and Behavior

In comparison with other Pacific salmon, the chum has the widest northern distribution. In the Arctic Ocean, its range extends from the Lena River in Siberia to the Mackenzie River and into the Northwest Territory's Great Bear Lake. Along the west coast, from Washington to Alaska, most major river systems have healthy runs of fish. Oddly, numerous attempts to establish the species elsewhere, such as along Ontario's James Bay coastline, have not been successful.

At sea, chum are distinguished from other salmon by their lack of distinct black spots along their backs, although they occasionally exhibit pale flecks. The only other Pacific salmon lacking dorsal spots – the sockeye – has a very small eye pupil, whereas the chum's is at least half the size of the eyeball.

As a chum salmon winds its way up a river to spawn, the steel blue hues on its back become dark olive, and its silver flanks turn pale green overlaid with an often-brilliant gray-purple flame pattern. These markings are especially prominent on males and serve as a sign of dominance in the competition for females.

The fish's spawning period is the shortest among salmon, and throughout their range, arrival time on the spawning beds varies extensively. In some rivers, fish begin running upstream in July, while in other streams the runs extend into January. Although primarily tidal spawners, rarely venturing more than 100 miles upstream, some strains of chum salmon may travel more than 1,000 miles. During their migration, they tend to hug the shoreline and stay in deep pools with slower currents and structure, like undercut banks and log jams.

Finding the Heavyweights

The average size of chum salmon appears to be largely dependent upon genetics. In some rivers, fish may average only 10 pounds, while other streams nearby may

IGFA RECORD

CHUM SALMON
Weight: 14.51 kg (32 lbs.)
Place: Behm Canal, Alaska, U.S.A.
Date: June 7, 1985
Angler: Frederick E. Thynes

produce fish twice that size. Any chum salmon over 20 pounds should be considered a trophy.

Fishing Techniques

In the ocean, particularly close to the river mouth, chum can be caught with the same baits and lures used for coho or chinook salmon. Trolling with spoons, hoochies, or plugs is the most common approach. In the lower stretches of a river, backtrolling from a drift boat with diving plugs, such as Kwikfish or Hot Shots, is an excellent way to locate moving fish. Anglers who wade in narrow, upper stretches of rivers or tributary streams will find spoons, spinners, or streamers highly effective.

Wow! This chum looks like the new world record!

Another beauty from the Skeena Valley in British Columbia.

HOT SPOT

Skeena Valley, British Columbia

There are many reasons that northern British Columbia is called big fish country, and the chum salmon is certainly one of them. Several 40-pound chum have come from the Terrace region, and Skeena River biologists have netted chum close to 50 pounds.

Sheltered by the mountains and glaciers of northern British Columbia, the Skeena River flows through the logging town of Terrace and spills into the Pacific Ocean at Prince Rupert. Only a limited number of guiding licenses have been issued to prevent overcrowding and preserve the quality of the sport fishery, but anglers can legally keep one chum per day.

Northwest Fishing Guides
Situated just north of Terrace, near the Kalum River, the lodge is operated by Northwest Fishing Guides, who have exclusive access to some of the finest salmon and steelhead water in British Columbia. With all modern conveniences, the lodge is fully equipped to entertain even the most discriminating angler.

ACCOMMODATIONS
• Main lodge

MEALS
• Breakfast
• Packed lunch or shore lunch
• Wine with dinner
• BYOB, honor bar

EQUIPMENT AVAILABLE
• Drift boats and jet boats
• Helicopter excursions
• Spinning and trolling tackle

RECOMMENDED EQUIPMENT
• Medium- or heavyweight fly rods with double handle, reels with good drags, eight- to 10- weight sinking line
• Leaders 12-17 pound test
• Streamers or roe imitations
• Medium- or medium-heavy-action rods from six to eight feet
• Bait-cast or spinning reels, 10- to 17-pound-test line, wire leader.
• Lures: single-hook spoons (like the Pixie), feathered or curly-tail jigs in bright colors.

SEASON
• March 15 to December
• Best fishing: August

CONTACT
Northwest Fishing Guides
P.O. Box 434
Terrace, British Columbia
V8G 4B1

HOT SPOT

Alaska

Yarntarni Camp
Outfitter Bill Martin offers a real wildness experience at the Yarntarni Camp, accessed via airplane from Anchorage. Besides catching trophy chum salmon, anglers will have the opportunity to catch coho salmon, pink salmon, and Dolly Varden.

ACCOMMODATIONS
• Camp with hot water, shower, and indoor plumbing
• For additional accommodations, inquire about Royal Coachman Lodge in Dillingham

EQUIPMENT AVAILABLE
• C-185 aircraft plus two four-wheel all-terrain vehicles to access the camp's five pristine rivers and streams
• Cook, guide, and pilot guide provided for eight guests per week

FISHING EQUIPMENT
• For smaller fish: an ultra-light spinning rod (four- to six-pound-test line) and a light fly rod (four or five weight).

• For chum, a seven- to nine-weight fly rod and a medium-action spinning rod with extra spools of eight- to 12-pound test.
• Flyfishermen should use short (six-foot) leaders.
• Mepps and Panther Martins are recommended spinning lures.

For seasons dates and other information, contact

Bill Martin's Fish Alaska
P.O. Box 450
Dillingham, Alaska 99576

Alaska Division of Tourism
P.O. Box 110801
Juneau, Alaska
99811-0801

Right: Their pronounced kype and sharp teeth have earned them the nickname "dog salmon."

Below: The vibrant green and purple bars are characteristic of spawning chums.

Coho Salmon

Scientific name: *Oncorhynchus kisutch*

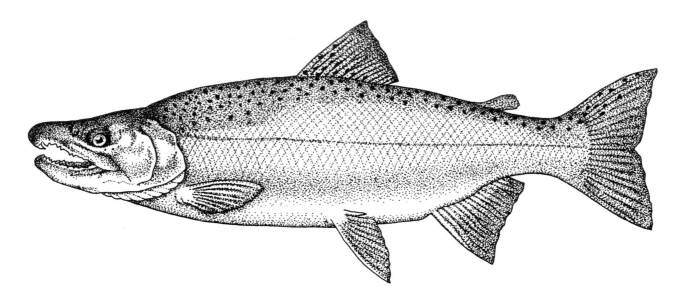

O riginally native
to the Pacific
coast of North
America from
California to Alaska, and
south again on the Asian side
as far as Japan, coho salmon
have been stocked widely
outside their natural range.
They sparked the dramatic
comeback of the Great Lakes
in the 1960s, and some have
even shown up on the
Atlantic coast of North
America – most likely strays
that wandered down the St.
Lawrence River from Great
Lakes stockings. But no matter where you find them,
they're magnificent gamefish.
Incredibly strong, relatively
abundant, and far from shy,
coho salmon can be goaded
into hitting a lure, which
makes for tremendously
exciting fishing.

Habitat and Behavior

Coho salmon spawn in cold,
clean, freshwater rivers from
September to February. Upon
hatching, the young remain
in the stream for almost 18
months before leaving for the
big water. In both the ocean
and the Great Lakes, cohos
are highly pelagic (preferring
the open water), seemingly
wandering at random, following squid and schools of
small fish. They seem to
spend most of their time suspended just under the surface, and track prey largely
by sight.

Since cohos travel in very
large, tight schools, when you
find one, you usually find a
bonanza. Occasionally you
hear of anglers running two
lures in tandem and hooking
two fish simultaneously.
Packs of hungry coho sometimes go into a feeding frenzy
and slash at anything that
moves.

In its third summer, a
coho can gain up to a pound
a week. By late summer, it
will return to the mouth of
its home river, where it continues to pack on weight
until cool rains send it
upstream. Most cohos enter
the rivers in prime silvery

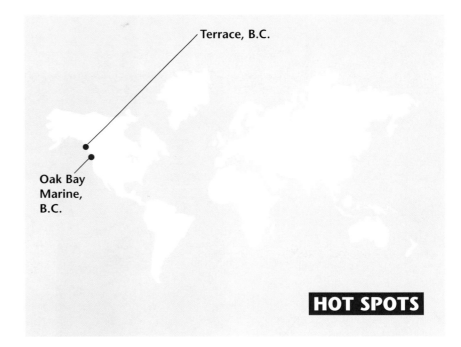

Terrace, B.C.

Oak Bay
Marine,
B.C.

HOT SPOTS

IGFA RECORD

COHO SALMON
Weight: 15.08 kg (33 lbs. 4 oz.)
Place: Salmon River, Pulaski, N.Y.
U.S.A.
Date: Sept. 27, 1989
Angler Jerry Lifton

condition, and provide tremendous fishing for shore fisherman or wading anglers. Indeed, fresh-run silvers are a favorite of flyfishermen. As they migrate upstream, cohos clear waterfalls and run incredible rapids, eventually working their way up even the tiniest spring creeks where they spawn and die. By the time they arrive in these locations, they darken into their spawning colors and gradually begin to decompose. Males often develop huge hooked snouts not unlike doorknobs, and vivid red sides with black backs, and female cohos turn dull olive to black, top and bottom. These spawning fish do not feed, but despite their deteriorated condition, they do not hesitate to attack

A trophy northern like this one would make any angler smile.

HOT SPOT

British Columbia Coast

The Oak Bay Marine Group operates six first-class fishing resorts along the British Columbia coast – three of them floating, mobile operations that go where the fishing is at its best. Trophy coho are a specialty and the prospects for a 20-pounder are excellent.

The angler has a broad choice of amenities, services, and price ranges to choose from. All six resorts offer outstanding accommodations, delicious meals, tackle, and top coho fishing.

ACCOMMODATIONS
• Six resorts

MEALS
• Full American Plan

EQUIPMENT AVAILABLE
• Modern boats with outboards

RECOMMENDED EQUIPMENT
• 10-foot mooching outfit with 20- to 25-pound-test line
• Medium-light spinning or bait-casting outfit
• Assortment of buzz bombs, jigging lures
• Assortment of spoons

SEASON
• Best fishing: July, August, and September

CONTACT
Oak Bay Marine Group
1327 Beach Drive
Victoria, British Columbia
V8S 2N4

smaller fish, each other, and even floating leaves. All cohos die shortly after spawning.

Finding the Heavyweights

Although the Great Lakes produce big coho, when it comes to catching quantities of trophy fish, the British Columbia coast remains the place to be. Thousands of anglers all along the Pacific rim wait eagerly for the annual return of the big "northerns" – prime coho up to and occasionally well over 20 pounds. These large, mature adults arrive on a predictable basis. The angler who times it right can catch a couple of 20-pound class coho in a morning. By comparison, trophy Great Lakes coho are needles in a very big haystack.

Hooking big cohos is one thing; landing them can be quite another. Hooked cohos seem to go in several different directions at once, including airborne. They're notorious for following retrieved baits and lures, only to hammer them right at the boat. The fish may dive, run just under the surface (with its tail and dorsal fin showing), or explode into a wild series of jumps, leaps, and tail walks. In the process, coho frequently wrap themselves up in the angler's line. Although their fight rarely lasts as long as that of the much larger chinook salmon, it is usually more violent. Just imagine 20 pounds of solid muscle that can swim 30 mph, turn on a dime, and twist like an Olympic gymnast.

Bringing a still-fresh coho into a small boat is always a bad idea. With most fish, the call for the net usually signals the end of the battle. But for the coho angler, the real fight has often just begun. Cohos to be kept should be killed at once before something gets broken or someone gets hurt. The fish are notorious for shaking their heads as anglers pry out hooks, accidentally impaling the unwary on their own lures. Cohos to be released shouldn't be brought into the boat at all. Pluck the hook out quickly with a pair of long-nosed pliers, or use a fish cradle to contain the coho at boatside.

Fishing Techniques

Cohos will attack just about anything that looks and acts

like a baitfish. Great Lakes anglers troll spoons, plugs, and dodger/fly combinations, usually with downriggers. West Coast fishermen mooch with bait or troll on the surface with big bucktails. Casting spoons or plugs also works well.

Catching fish in rivers can be a bit tougher. Small spinners or banana plugs, like the Kwikfish, account for numerous cohos. Other anglers drift roe imitations, like yarn or plastic eggs. Most roe colors produce well, but forest green seems to work best.

HOT SPOT

British Columbia

The best time to catch a trophy Pacific coho is in August and September. These big, thick-bodied fish, which B.C. anglers refer to as northerns, have spent the summer feeding off Alaska. They frequently top 20 pounds, but 15 to 18 pounds is considered a good catch.

NORTHWEST FISHING GUIDES
It's great catching a trophy coho in open water, but it's twice as exciting in a river; that's the specialty of Northwest Fishing Guides. Situated near the Kalum River just north of Terrace, this location provides access to some of the finest salmon waters in British Columbia.

ACCOMMODATION
• Main lodge

MEALS
• Full American Plan

EQUIPMENT AVAILABLE
• Drift boats and jet boats
• Spinning, trolling and fly-fishing gear

SEASON
• August to October
• Best fishing: August

CONTACT
Northwest Fishing Guides
P.O. Box 434
Terrace, British Columbia
V8G 4B1

What else can be said about gorgeous holding pools like this one?

This male coho shows off his pronounced kype.

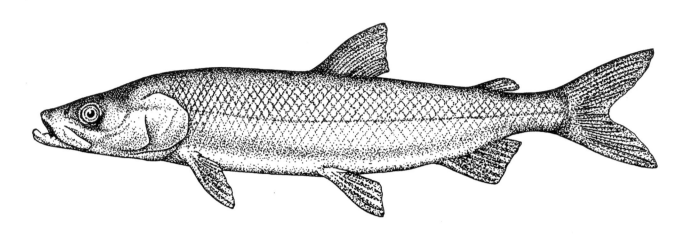

Inconnu

Scientific name: *Stenodus leucichthys*

No gamefish is more aptly labeled than the elusive inconnu, or sheefish. *Inconnu* is a French word meaning "unknown." And the inconnu is a fish of unspoiled northern lakes and rivers. To find it, one must fly to the top of North America, to the Yukon and Alaska. No other freshwater gamefish is so inaccessible to anglers.

The inconnu may be mysterious, but few gamefish provide such exciting sport. With a superficial resemblance to the tarpon, in both appearance and fighting qualities, the inconnu runs with authority and jumps repeatedly, often clearing the water by several feet. It requires skill, stout tackle, and more than a bit of luck to bring this tough customer to hand.

The inconnu is the largest member of the whitefish family, which, along with the trout and salmon, are members of the Salmonidae family. At first glance, it looks like a cross between a cisco and a

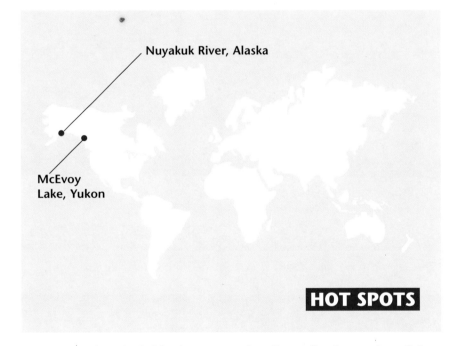

Nuyakuk River, Alaska

McEvoy Lake, Yukon

HOT SPOTS

tarpon, with a dark black back, silvery sides, and a white belly. The most distinctive feature is its large, upturned, tarpon-like mouth.

The inconnu's streamlined body is perfectly shaped for long-distance travel. Indeed, inconnu regularly migrate distances of more than 930 miles.

Habitat and Behavior

The inconnu is the only member of the whitefish

family to feed on other fish. Its sheer size makes it a formidable predator that feeds mostly on other whitefish, minnows, and even small pike. In Alaska it is believed that inconnu travel up into rivers to intercept salmon fingerlings migrating downstream. Such a rich diet inevitably packs the pounds onto these fish.

The inconnu is native to Alaska and northwestern Canada. Although it is prized as a superior gamefish, its small home range and limited availability have discouraged attempts to stock it in other bodies of water. It tends to school in both lake and river habitats.

Finding the Heavyweights

Most inconnu range in size from six to 12 pounds, but fish of 20 pounds and better are commonly caught by anglers. There is considerable evidence to support the claim of a 63-pounder caught at the mouth of the MacKenzie River in 1936, and anglers have reported other inconnu from that area between 45 and 55 pounds. Inconnu to 55 pounds have also been reported from the Great Slave Lake drainage.

Fishing Techniques

Inconnu are eagerly sought by both spin fishermen and fly casters. Anglers often try to intercept schools of fish as they migrate along rivers and streams, or at spots where they congregate in lakes. Aircraft are often used to locate schools of inconnu as they make their way along rivers or in lake systems. Base camps are then set up

IGFA RECORD

INCONNU
Weight: 24.04 kg (53 lbs.)
Place: Pah River, Alaska, U.S.A.
Date: Aug. 20, 1986
Angler: Lawrence E. Hudnall

The inconnu has a limited range but is highly prized as a gamefish.

HOT SPOT

Yukon Territory

The combination of vast tundra, mountain peaks, and alpine plateaus makes this area one of the most beautiful places on earth to fish.

Inconnu Lodge
Based in the southern Yukon's McEvoy Lake, Inconnu Lodge offers fly-out trips to nearby rivers, streams, and lakes for world-class inconnu fishing. Located on the continental divide, 185 miles east of the town of Whitehorse, Inconnu Lodge accommodates up to 20 guests in relaxed comfort. Travel to the fishing areas is by air, using both fixed-wind aircraft and a helicopter.

ACCOMMODATIONS
• Rooms with private shower/washrooms
• Sauna/hot tub

MEALS
• Full American Plan
• Lounge

EQUIPMENT AVAILABLE
• Boats and canoes

RECOMMENDED EQUIPMENT
• Waders are recommended for stream fishing
• Light to medium spinning or baitcasting outfits; line from six- to 20-pound test.
• Assorted plugs, spinners, spoons, extra line, spare hooks
• Six- to nine-weight fly tackle, with both floating and sinking tip/sinking lines
• Assorted wet and dry flies, weighted nymphs

SEASON
• Lodge open from June 15 to September 15.
• Best fishing: July

CONTACT:
Inconnu Lodge
Box 4730
Whitehorse, Yukon Territory
Y1A 4N6

Migration up the rivers of Alaska and northern Canada occurs in June and July.

so anglers can stay within easy reach of the fish.

Once a school is located, persistence and dedication are called for. The adventurous angler will walk great distances along a river, making cast after cast. Hardware-tossers need carry only a limited selection of spinners, spoons, plugs, and jigs to tempt the inconnu. Anything flashy that resembles a smaller fish will attract them. Remember, these fish rarely,

if ever, see fishing lures.

When you fish along rivers, the strength of the current will dictate tackle selection. Slower pools can be easily fished with light lures. To catch inconnu holding in small pockets of slack water surrounded by swift current, heavy lures like $1/2$- to 1-ounce spoons and jigs are the best choice.

Fly anglers face a greater challenge. In the spring, inconnu will feed on the surface, making dry flies a number-one choice. In summer or early fall, when these fish are more apt to lie low near the bottom, a sinking line or a sink-tip with a medium- to fast-sinking braided leader is the best approach. Powerful nine-weight outfits coupled with flashy streamer flies will usually yield results. Of course a strong casting arm is also a benefit for making repeated casts in search of active fish.

The inconnu is a prize fighter, similar to a tarpon, except it's a freshwater fish.

HOT SPOT

Alaska

The lakes and rivers of the breath-taking Alaskan frontier are prime locations for inconnu. Flying in on a float plane just adds to the experience.

Royal Coachman Lodge
Located in southwest Alaska, Royal Coachman Lodge offers some of the world's most exciting fishing for inconnu. Just 60 miles north of the town of Dillingham, the camp sits an the outlet of the Tikchik Lakes, on the Nuyakuk Watershed. Daily flyout fishing allows easy access to remote streams, rivers, and lakes. In addition to trophy inconnu, 12 other species are available during your wilderness adventure.

Royal Coachman Lodge accommodates up to 12 guests at a time. The rustic main lodge features a large dining area, wet bar, and lounge. Home-cooked meals keep your energy up.

ACCOMMODATIONS
• Main lodge building and comfort-able cabins with private baths
• Lounge area, dining room

MEALS
• Full American Plan

EQUIPMENT AVAILABLE
• Flights to remote lakes and streams
• Jet boats for local fishing

RECOMMENDED EQUIPMENT
• Medium-heavy spinning or bait-casting outfit with 12- to 20-pound-test line.
• An ultra-light outfit, with four- to six-pound test, makes catching the smaller fish much more fun
• Assortment of spinners, spoons, and crankbaits.
• Four- to five-weight fly outfit with floating line
• Nine-weight fly outfit, with a fast sinking line
• Weighted wet flies.

SEASON
• Best fishing: July

CONTACT
Bill Martin's Fish Alaska
P.O. Box 450
Dillingham, Alaska
99576

Lake Trout

Scientific name: *Salvelinus namaycus*

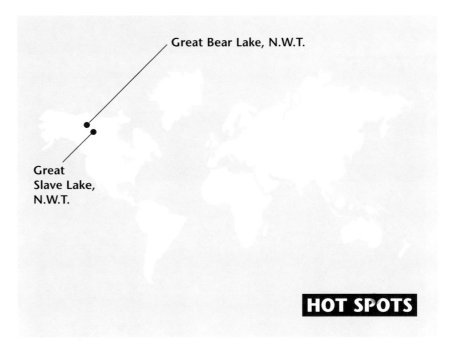

The majestic queen of Canada's cold, clear, northern waters is the lake trout. Not only is this denizen of the depths plentiful throughout Canada, it also grows to monstrous proportions. Occasionally topping 60 pounds, the laker is master of its domain.

Lake trout offer anglers the best of two worlds. Smaller, eager fish are plentiful enough to provide light tackle sport – and a tasty northern shore lunch – while larger lake trout provide a "big game" experience. Tangling with a 30-pound-plus behemoth is enough to get any angler's adrenaline flowing.

Although called a trout, this fish is actually a member of the char family. Like other char, its body bears a pattern of light spots over a dark background, with brilliantly hued lower fins marked with striking orange and red rays, preceded by a slash of white on the leading rays of the pectoral, pelvic, and anal fins.

Great Bear Lake, N.W.T.

Great Slave Lake, N.W.T.

HOT SPOTS

Habitat and Behavior

Lake trout in small lakes often feed on plankton, freshwater crustaceans, and aquatic insects. Larger lake trout and those found in larger bodies of water will feed on other fish. They prefer ciscoes, but will eat any available prey, including smelt and alewives.

The natural distribution of lake trout closely follows the limits of the Pleistocene glaciation, which occurred in most of Canada, and takes in the Great Lakes and in the northern reaches of the midwestern and northeastern United States. Lake Trout have been transplanted to other parts of the U.S., as well as New Zealand, South America, and Sweden.

Finding the Heavyweights

What qualifies as a trophy-sized lake trout varies with the size of the body of water.

In small lakes, where fish may feed almost exclusively on plankton and aquatic insects, the size of a trophy laker approximates that of its close cousin, the brook trout – five or six pounds is usually tops. The real heavyweights require big water and a large forage base. The Great Lakes, lakes Nipigon and Temagami in Ontario, lakes Waterbury and Athabasca in Saskatchewan and of course Great Bear and Great Slave lakes in the Northwest Territories all provide the right conditions for monster lakers.

Fishing Techniques

Trophy lake trout are caught using a variety of standard casting and trolling techniques. Getting the lure in front of the fish is often the biggest challenge.

In most areas, lake trout anglers search for water 80 to 100 feet deep where the cold-loving lakers escape the sun's warmth. The best lakes for lake trout have substantial areas of bottom where trout can find water of just above 40°F, along with bottom structure like deep breaks and dropoffs, and

Many big lakers are taken on a jig-and-sucker-meat combo.

IGFA RECORD

LAKE TROUT
Weight: 30.16 kg (66 lbs. 8 oz.)
Place: Great Bear Lake, N.W.T., Canada
Date: July 19, 1991
Angler: Rodney Harback

HOT SPOT

Great Bear Lake, Northwest Territories

There's no question – if you want a trophy lake trout, Great Bear Lake in Canada's Northwest Territories is the place to go. Each year, many seasoned anglers who visit Great Bear claim to have hooked and lost fish bigger than the current record of 66^1/$_2$ pounds!

Plummer's Lodge
Plummer's Lodge recently moved from the south shore of Great Bear Lake to a point on the remote northeast side, 47 miles above the Arctic circle, adjacent to the famed Dease Arm – one of the most productive lake-trout waters in the world.

ACCOMMODATIONS
• Main lodge building with detached cabins
• Living room area, modern plumbing, electricity, showers, oil heat, laundry service available

MEALS
• Full American Plan
• Morning coffee at your door

• Shore lunches available

EQUIPMENT AVAILABLE
• 18-foot aluminium boats with swivel seats
• 25-hp outboards with four hp backup

RECOMMENDED EQUIPMENT
• Heavy spinning or baitcasting outfit with 12- to 17-pound-test line
• Light spinning outfit with eight-pound-test line
• Eight- or nine-weight fly outfit with sinking lines
• Large spoons, diving crankbaits, jigs
• Large streamer flies

SEASON
• Lodge season: July and August
• Best fishing: July and August

CONTACT
Plummer's
950 Bradford Street
Winnipeg, Manitoba
R3H 0N5

plenty of small forage fish.

The traditional way to get a lure down to bottom-hugging lakers is to troll with wire or steel line. The original rig for this was a short, stout rod with a huge, oversized single-action reel, more like a small bicycle wheel. Modern anglers may still use steel line, but today it is more likely to be spooled on a high-capacity baitcasting outfit.

Wire-line outfits offer lake-trout anglers several advantages. No matter how much weight is attached to monofilament, it never sinks as fast as wire. Wire is thin in diameter, which allows lower water resistance and greater reel capacity, and it is virtually stretch-free, which makes solid hooksets possible even with great lengths of line out. And since wire is also relatively cheap, financial losses are not great when (not if) it inevitably snags the bottom.

Starting in the late 1960s, anglers began experimenting with downriggers for lake trout. Downriggers are like miniature winches attached to a heavy weight that hangs below the boat. Just above the weight is a quick-release mechanism, to which a fishing line is attached. Most come with some sort of counter to indicate the depth of the weight. If your fish finder indicates fish at 89 feet, you simply lower the downrigger until the counter reads 89 feet.

Downriggers are so precise that they allow anglers to skirt the edges of underwater trenches and drops without hanging up continually. They also allow the use of light tackle, because once the fish hits and pulls the line free of the release, it's just the angler and the fish, with no added weight on the line. Anglers can even troll with light fly rods in this fashion.

Of course the approach must be different in cold northern lakes where lake trout may cruise just under the surface year-round. Trolling, jigging, and casting are all productive methods for catching shallow-water lake trout. The biggest ones are most often caught by trolling huge plugs or spoons.

Trolling is not the only approach. Anglers catch plenty of lake trout by jigging over deep shoals using spoons or jigs as heavy as two ounces. Tipping the jig with a piece of fish – usually a strip cut from the belly of a sucker or whitefish – helps. Big white or yellow twister tails, as well as minnow-imitating rubber jigs, are other proven lake trout favorites.

Big lake trout that cruise into shallow waters can often be caught by sight casting using a variety of spoons, plugs, and spinners.

HOT SPOT

Great Slave Lake, Northwest Territories

While nearby Great Bear Lake receives most of the press with its famed record catches, Great Slave has quietly been producing trophy lakers of its own. Seasoned anglers who have fished both bodies of water consider it a toss-up which lake will produce the next world record.

Frontier Fishing Lodge
Located 115 miles east of Yellowknife on the east arm of Great Slave Lake, at the mouth of the Stark River, Frontier Fishing Lodge is a modern, comfortable facility catering to anglers in quest of Great Slave's trophy lake trout.

ACCOMMODATIONS
• Main lodge with six bedrooms
• Log cabins
• Conference area with seven attached bedrooms

MEALS
• Breakfast
• Lunch
• Dinner

EQUIPMENT AVAILABLE
• Aluminium fishing boats with outboards

RECOMMENDED EQUIPMENT
• Flexible trolling rod, six to seven feet long

• Heavy baitcasting or flipping rod with 17- to 35-pound-test line
• Medium-light spinning outfit with six- to eight-pound-test line
• Eight- or nine-weight fly outfit with floating and sinking lines
• Large spoons, trolling plugs
• Large streamers

SEASON
• Lodge open: mid-June to mid-September
• Best fishing: June and July

CONTACT
Frontier Fishing Lodge
5515 – 82 Avenue
Edmonton, Alberta T6B 2J6

Largemouth Bass

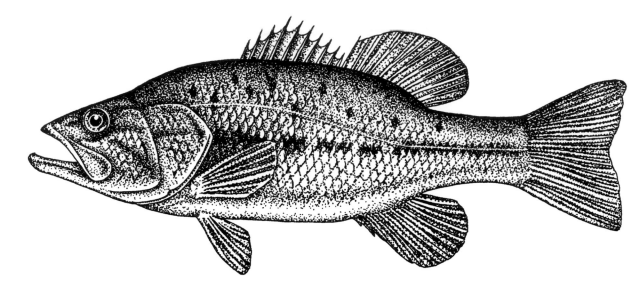

Scientific name: *Micropterus salmoides*

"**B**ucketmouth." "Hawg." "Ol' moss back." These and other pet names pepper any discussion about largemouth bass. No matter what folks call them, more people in North America fish for largemouth bass than any other species of freshwater fish. In the United States, relatively good largemouth fishing can be found in almost any lake or river. But even in the walleye country of southeastern Canada, the largemouth ranks high with many anglers.

The largemouth has spawned a large competitive fishing industry in North America. Each year, competitions award millions of dollars to anglers who catch the largest or most largemouth bass in a given time. Individual anglers rise to celebrity status and earn hundreds of thousands of dollars, much like professional golfers and tennis players. The pursuit of largemouth bass is so popular that it has even spawned the largest fishing society on the continent – the

Bass Angler Sportsman Society (B.A.S.S.), which airs an international television series focusing on bass fishing. Thousands of anglers tune in weekly to see how the big fish are caught so they can emulate their bass-fishing heroes and put some "hawgs" in the boat themselves. There is even a "bass language" that includes phrases like "flippin'," "pitchin'," and "crankin'" to describe various fishing techniques.

Analyzing the largemouth's enormous popularity is difficult, since they're not elusive, tough to catch, or particularly big. Still, they have a charm all their own, and they rank high in the hearts of millions of anglers.

Largemouths are generally greenish in color, combining a dark green or black back fading to medium green flanks with a whitish belly. You can easily tell a largemouth from the closely related smallmouth bass by the dark-colored horizontal band

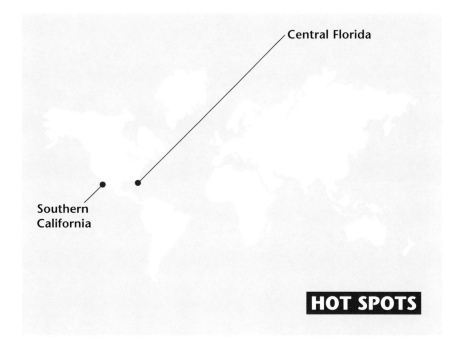

Central Florida

Southern California

HOT SPOTS

IGFA RECORD

LARGEMOUTH BASS
Weight: 10.09 kg (22 lbs. 4 oz.)
Place: Montgomery Lake, Georgia,
U.S.A.
Date: June 2, 1932
Angler: George W. Perry

With warm waters and an extended season, the southern United States produces some of the largest bass in the world.

running the length of the largemouth's body near the lateral line. The largemouth really does have a large mouth, especially in relation the size of the whole fish. When the mouth is closed, the upper jawbone extends back well past the eye, whereas a smallmouth's jaw barely reaches the eye.

Habitat and Behavior

Largemouth bass are indigenous to much of southeastern North America, from just north of the Great Lakes/St. Lawrence River basin west to beyond the Mississippi drainage system. Their popularity has now increased their distribution to include almost every state (including Hawaii), parts of western Canada, and internationally to Japan, Hong Kong, Brazil, the Philippines, England, and South Africa.

Largemouths favor shallow, warm, weedy lakes and slow-moving rivers. However, partly as a result of extensive stocking programs that have spread largemouths well beyond their natural range, it is possible to catch them in a variety of situations. Most fish stay in water less than 20 feet deep. Typical largemouth habitat includes marshy bays and coves, stump-filled lakes and streams, boat docks, and other such physical structures in shallow water. They are supreme opportunists, and will not hesitate to feed suspended in open water. Indeed, numerous catches from California nearing the world record of 22 pounds four ounces have been made by anglers fishing in very deep water that would seem out of character for largemouths.

The largemouth's bucket of a mouth takes in a variety of small fish, crustaceans, frogs, snakes, swimming mice, birds, ducklings, and all sorts of other suitably sized creatures. There isn't much a largemouth won't try to eat, and accounts of bass choking to death while

HOT SPOT

Southern California

If any area was to give Florida a run for its money as a potential record bass producer, it would have to be southern California and its ultra-clear reservoirs. These waters have produced more near-record largemouth bass than any other area in the world.

Lake Castaic near Los Angeles and other southern California reservoirs aren't even native ground for largemouth. They were stocked with large-mouths from Florida. But the fish have done well, feeding on stocked rainbow trout, and establishing amazing growth rates even bass biologists find baffling.

Largemouth fishing in southern California reservoirs is a unique experience. Anglers here catch big bass by fishing deep, sunken structures (like rock piles) – especially those with schools of suspended trout nearby. The techniques vary, from fishing with small live baits (crayfish are tops) and light line, to trolling with crankbaits, to jigging.

With the bustling city of San Diego just a short drive away, anglers visiting Lake Castaic and other southern California bass reservoirs will have little trouble finding accommodations, which range from luxurious to basic. In addition, fishing guides, boat rentals, bait, and tackle are all readily available.

CONTACT
San Diego Chamber of Commerce
402 W. Broadway, Suite 1000
San Diego, California 92101

attempting to swallow another bass of the same size are not unusual.

Finding the Heavyweights

For all the hoopla, largemouth bass are not really big fish. Their average size is usually about two pounds. Exactly what constitutes a trophy largemouth is determined largely by geographic location. For example, a five-pound bass is considered a genuine trophy in southern Canada, where long winters make for a short growing season. In areas like Florida, where the fish grow all year, it takes a 10-pounder to be considered a trophy, and fish in the mid-teens are caught every year. Although less heavily fished areas like Cuba or Central America do grow very large bass, it seems that these waters are simply too warm. Because of the bass's increased metabolism in the hot water, the fish literally burn themselves out at a young age. Although Cuban lakes produce scores of five- to seven-pound fish, very few largemouths over 10 pounds have been reported.

Fishing Techniques

The general rule is that the bigger the lure or bait, the bigger the bass you will catch, but in the clear reservoirs of California, which have given up some of the biggest bass in recent history, smaller, more subtle lures (like four-inch-long plastic worms or grubs) have been very successful. The best tactic is to try to match the size of the available forage. If bass feed on large leeches, use big plastic worms. If they dine on tiny shiners, smaller minnow plugs will likely produce best.

Standard tactics for big largemouths just about anywhere in their range include

Prime bucketmouth territory – flooded timber and weeds.

fishing with plastic worms, crankbaits, top water baits, or flipping jigs.

Flipping heavy cover with weedless jigs is one of the deadliest techniques known. Flipping takes advantage of the largemouth's habit of burying into the deepest cover around. As a rule, the biggest bass tend to inhabit the least-accessible spots. Anglers flip heavy cover areas by lobbing a weedless, rubber-skirted jig underhand into open pockets, beside logs or into downed trees. Bass in these spots tend to hit fearlessly. Hooking the fish is the easy part; hauling it out of a heavy underwater jungle is difficult and requires very heavy tackle and line. Most anglers go with heavy-action, two-handed baitcasting rods in the seven-foot range, with heavy reels and line up to and over 25-pound test. It's hard to imagine needing 25-pound-test line for a fish that

HOT SPOT

Florida

The next world-record bass could easily come from the state of Florida, particularly the central area known as the Ocala National Forest. A number of factors contribute to its potential: it is loaded with small, shallow, fertile lakes with more than enough forage to feed a big bass; the climate is favorable, with a year-round growing season, and many of the lakes are remote enough to have

escaped the fishing pressure of many other southern waters.

Lakes and rivers in this area continue to produce mammoth largemouth bass. Anglers bent on catching a big Florida bass are advised to contact local guides and plan their trip to coincide with the prime fishing period. Since conditions change each year, good local contacts mean everything.

Finding suitable accommodations in Florida is the easiest part of any trip there, since tourism is a major industry. For detailed information on accommodations and largemouth-bass guides, contact

Florida Department of Commerce
Room 505, Collins Building
107 W. Gaines,
Tallahassee, Florida 32399-2000

might weigh six pounds – until you've tried landing big bass in heavy cover on anything less.

Live bait is also popular with big bass hunters. In the southern United States, fishing with huge eight- to

12-inch golden shiners suspended under a balloon float produces some of the biggest bass. Many of the biggest bass from California have been caught using live crayfish. Frogs are another good big bass bait.

A young angler displays his eight-pound trophy bass.

Ten pounds of Okeechobee bass.

Muskellunge

Scientific name: *Esox masquinongy*

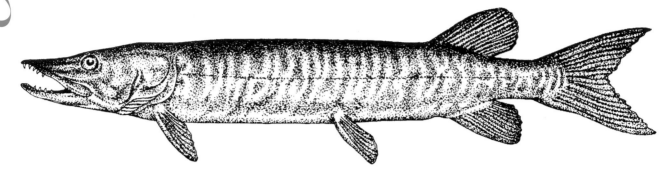

No other freshwater predatory fish is more widely revered than the mighty muskellunge. Anglers who fish for muskies are not just ordinary anglers; they're die-hards who brave rough water, snow squalls, and torturous, cold November winds in search of one of the biggest freshwater fish in North America.

Wherever the muskie roams, it is king of its domain. It fears no other fish and many anglers will attest that it has no fear of humans either. The muskie is legendary for its great size and the ferocity with which it strikes a bait. Only after hooking one's first muskie can one truly comprehend why this fish creates such a dedicated following. Words cannot do justice to the powerful thrust of this fish or its acrobatic leaps and cartwheels.

As the largest member of the pike family, the muskellunge has a long, lean, and very muscular body with a large tail. Both the dorsal and anal fins are located well to the rear. Most muskies have light silver to gray/green flanks with a darker back and light-colored belly, and may be easily distinguished from large pike by the fact they have light bodies with dark markings – just the opposite of pike. Muskellunge from different parts of their range show highly variable color patterns. For instance, Great Lakes muskies tend to have silvery flanks peppered with golf-ball-sized dark green or black blotches, while fish from the Ohio Valley display prominent vertical bars. Although the International Game Fish Association deems all muskies one and the same, many scientists argue that at least three different subspecies may exist.

Habitat and Behavior

The muskellunge is found in the fresh waters of Canada from southern Quebec, including the St. Lawrence

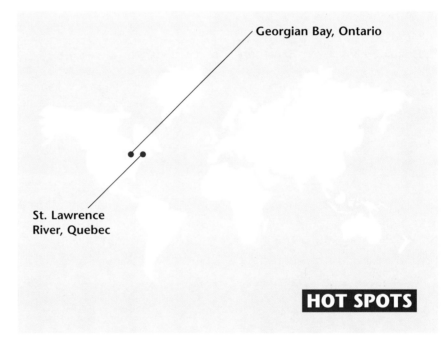

Georgian Bay, Ontario

St. Lawrence River, Quebec

HOT SPOTS

River, through south and central Ontario and into the southern part of Manitoba; and in the United States, throughout the upper Midwest. Its eastern border runs in a line from Vermont southwest down to Tennessee. The edge of its distribution includes Wisconsin, Minnesota, Ohio, New York, and Pennsylvania.

The muskellunge can be found in a variety of lakes and large river habitats. It favors shallow fertile lakes with heavy weed cover, logs, and other shallow water structures. In large bodies of water, it will inhabit water as deep as 50 feet. In fact, many dedicated muskie hunters will fish only in water deeper than 20 feet because of the general belief that the biggest muskies are to be found in the deepest water.

The muskie's apparently insatiable appetite spawns legends wherever this fish is found. Taxidermists still report finding enormous items, including trophy bass and walleye, ducklings, full-grown teal, and even muskrats, in the gullets of trophy muskies.

Finding the Heavyweights

The muskellunge draws a following for two reasons: its sheer size and the ferocity of its fight when hooked. The average-sized muskie weighs about 10 pounds, and even at this size the fish provides absolutely gut-wrenching action. Indeed, after tangling with a 10-pounder you'll find it hard to imagine battling a 30-pounder.

Although huge muskies are available all through its home

IGFA RECORD

MUSKELLUNGE
Weight: 29.48 kg (65 lbs.)
Place: Blackstone Harbour, Ontario, Canada
Date: Oct. 16, 1988
Angler: Kenneth J. O'Brien

A big 50-pounder, big smiles, on a big river, the St. Lawrence.

HOT SPOT

Georgian Bay, Ontario

Georgian Bay, and in particular its Moon River Basin area, has drawn a lot of attention over the past few years for the huge muskies it produces. This area has everything going for it – cover, structure, miles of water, an enormous forage base, including whitefish up to 10 pounds, and a strong population of fast-growing, long-lived wild muskies that are genetically different from any other muskies in the world. Little wonder then that Georgian Bay continues to produce muskies well over 50 pounds. Although many waters can beat the big bay when it comes to quantity, no other lake or river on earth can top it when it comes to producing big fish.

Georgian Bay muskies are strictly loners. To catch one, you have to put in a lot of hours covering a lot of ground.

The eastern shoreline of Georgian Bay, including the Moon River Basin, bristles with fishing lodges ranging from rustic camps to plush five-star resorts. The best muskie guides are often booked up to a full year in advance, so careful planning well ahead of time is essential.

For information on Georgian Bay muskie fishing, contact

Georgian Lakelands Travel Association
P.O. Box 39
Orillia, Ontario L3V 6H9

This classic trophy was caught from shore on a yellow jig.

range, the biggest specimens are common to the larger bodies of water. Georgian Bay, Lake of the Woods, Eagle Lake, and the border waters of the St. Lawrence River are legendary big-muskie waters in Canada. Famous U.S. locations include the St. Lawrence River and Chautauqua Lake in New York, the Chippewa Flowage in Wisconsin, Leech Lake in Minnesota, and the St. Clair River in Michigan.

Fishing Techniques

A variety of techniques are used to catch big muskies, from casting to trolling to still-fishing with live or dead bait. Although muskie fanatics generally concentrate on the fall months, muskies are available throughout the spring, summer, and fall. Depending on local regulations, muskies usually are ready for a fight in late spring just after spawning. At this time of the year, the fish are usually shallow and will concentrate along the edges of heavy cover or near drop-offs associated with shallow feeding flats. Veteran anglers choose big flashy spinnerbaits or oversized in-line spinners like the Mepps Muskie Killer. As summer progresses, trophy hunters switch to trolling big-bodied baits like the Believer or Swim Whizz. Prime locations for truly huge fish are areas along steep dropping points near large feeding flats.

Fall is prime muskie time. At this time, muskies will move closer to shallow feeding flats in order to fatten up for the oncoming winter. It is at this time that the fish will attack surface baits. One of the best techniques is jerk baiting, which involves using a class of lures known as jerk baits that are cast out and jerked back in. Muskie veterans use short stout rods loaded with 20- to 30-pound-test line and jerk baits ranging in size from nine to 24 inches. Big lures mean big fish!

Below: Large bucktail spinners are top producers.

Bottom: The persistent and patient angler will eventually be rewarded.

HOT SPOT
St. Lawrence River

Second only to Georgian Bay as a producer of enormous muskellunge, the mighty St. Lawrence River, which drains the Great Lakes into the Atlantic, was at one time the undisputed muskie capital of the world. Numerous muskies in excess of 50 pounds have been caught here, including a handful of fish over 60 pounds.

Like Georgian Bay, the St. Lawrence has habitat, forage, and a unique wild population of muskies that consistently reach record-book proportions. And like Georgian Bay, it has a long and honored muskie-fishing heritage.

Muskie are most plentiful from Lake Ontario downstream to Montreal. Accommodations and guides are readily available at any of the riverside towns, particularly on the Canadian side. As always, the best guides are booked far in advance. For season dates and other information, contact

Eastern Ontario Travel
Association
209 Ontario Street
Kingston, Ontario K7L 2Z1

Federation of Québec Outfitters
2485 boul. Hamel
Québec City, Quebec G1P 2H9

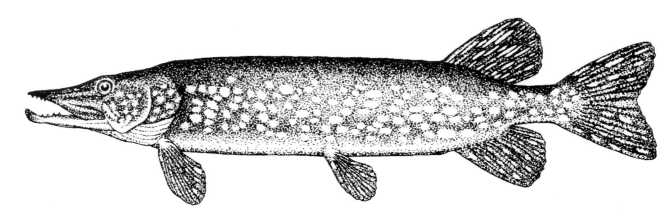

Northern Pike

Scientific name: *Esox lucius*

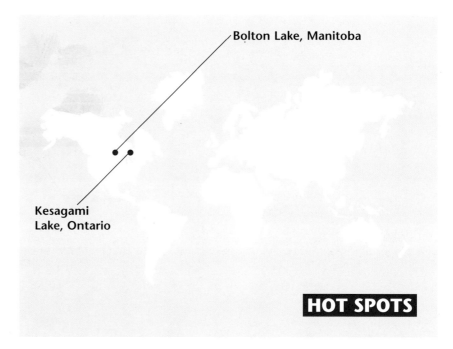

Bolton Lake, Manitoba

Kesagami
Lake, Ontario

HOT SPOTS

The northern pike is one of nature's predatory marvels. Aggressive and voracious, it will not hesitate to attack anything of reasonable size that moves. A wide variety of items grace its menu, including fish, amphibians, reptiles, birds, and even small mammals. The fearless pike has even been known to attack fish of its own size, and legion are the stories of finding a dead pike that choked while trying to swallow another only slightly smaller. No wonder this ruthless predator has often been described as a freshwater eating machine.

The pike's sinister-looking head and lean, torpedo-like body have intrigued people for centuries and have inspired myths of pike of mammoth proportions. If mystery and sheer size are enough to stir the angler's imagination, the pike is certainly well qualified. Indeed, few things are more exciting than a 20-pound pike single-mindedly intent on attacking the angler's lure.

Habitat and Behavior

The northern pike is an enormously successful species that is widely distributed throughout the world, including all over Canada, the northern regions of the United States (including Alaska), Siberia, Europe, and Scandinavia. Although a freshwater species, northerns have managed to survive in waters with a low salt content, and may be caught in semi-brackish water in some areas of Europe.

Pike are also one of the fastest-growing freshwater fish. Some pike have reportedly grown at the astonishing rate of 15 inches in only four months. Once they reach adulthood, pike are almost entirely piscivorous. The most common items found in the stomachs of captured pike are ciscoes, suckers, and a variety of panfish such as bluegills, crappies, or yellow perch. Pike will, nevertheless, devour any fish species

IGFA RECORD

NORTHERN PIKE
Weight: 25 kg (55 lbs. 1 oz.)
Place: Lake of Grefeern, Germany
Date: Oct. 16, 1986
Angler: Lothar Louis

they can swallow. These may include some of the angler's favorite gamefish, including walleyes, brook trout, and bass.

Finding the Heavyweights

Pike perform all their carnivorous deeds in daylight and are known to anglers as one of the most reliable "hitters" of all freshwater gamefish. Very large pike, on the other hand, are quite unpredictable. One theory suggests that lunker pike have learned to feed on larger prey, and do not need to feed as frequently as their smaller kin. The angler must therefore attempt to appeal to a big fish that has not recently enjoyed a big meal. The most dependable time to encounter large, ravenous pike is shortly after spawning, when they are accessible in shallow water and will most likely have empty stomachs. The best time of day to hunt trophy

The northern pike is one of the fastest-growing freshwater fish.

pike is early morning or late afternoon – their favorite feeding times.

Fishing Techniques

The key to enticing the heavyweights is to use large baits. There are, of course, numerous lure types in this category, including spinner-baits, in-line spinners, body baits, and spoons. Jigs in the $1/2$- to $3/4$-ounce size range are particularly effective when precise casting is necessary.

Anglers can also target big pike that cruise along weed lines or the edges of heavy

Top left: The duck-bill jaws of the northern pike contain large, sharp-pointed teeth.

Left: Mesh cradles come in handy when releasing large northerns like this 25-pounder.

HOT SPOT

Kesagami Lake, Ontario

Kesagami Lake, in northern Ontario's Kesagami Provincial Park, has recently emerged as a big pike heaven, with trophies up to 28 pounds. The average pike runs about six pounds, but in 1993 one out of every three anglers boated a 20-pounder, and just about every-one boated a 15-pounder.

Access to the park is by air only. Kesagami Wilderness Lodge, the only outfitter in the park, caters specifically to anglers in quest of big pike. The lake also offers excel-lent fishing for eating-sized

walleyes – one of the reasons it holds so many big pike.

Kesagami is a shallow lake averag-ing just seven feet deep. You find pike along shoreline structure breaks, in shallow bays, or along the edges of offshore weed beds.

Kesagami Wilderness Lodge
Kesagami Wilderness Lodge is a full-service establishment with accommodation in cabins or the main lodge building.

ACCOMMODATIONS
• Housekeeping and American Plan cabins, with showers in main lodge building
• Main lodge rooms with private shower and bath

MEALS
• Breakfast
• Lunch (shore lunches or packed

lunches available)
• Dinner
• Guest lounge and recreation area

EQUIPMENT AVAILABLE
• 23-foot boats with outboards

RECOMMENDED EQUIPMENT
• Heavy-action spinning and bait-casting outfits with 20-pound-test line
• Eight- or nine-weight fly tackle
• Wire leaders a must
• Top lures: T16 Kwikfish, large jointed Rapalas, jerk baits, large spoons, inline spinners, large jigs

SEASON
• May to August
• Best fishing: June and July

CONTACT
Kesagami Wilderness Lodge
371 Airport Road North
Naples, Florida 33942

cover, including weed beds, submerged timber, and rock piles. Trolling or casting with large plugs, such as Kwikfish or Rapalas, along the cover edge attracts big fish.

Bait fishermen can also capitalize on the big pike's voracious, if somewhat unpredictable, feeding habits. Again, relatively large baits are required. Live or dead baitfish (preferably soft-finned fish such as suckers) are fished on the bottom on slip-sinker rigs, or suspended under a substantial float, along the same cover edges. The difficult part of baitfishing is determining when to set the hook. Pike will usually grab a bait and dash off on a short run, then stop to turn the bait so it can be more easily swallowed (hence the reason for slip sinkers). Seasoned anglers wait until the fish stops before setting the hook. Other anglers opt for "quick strike" rigs, which involve two or more hooks positioned along the length of the bait. With this set-up, there is always at least one hook in the pike's mouth, and a hook can be set as soon as the fish picks up the bait.

Whether baitfishing or using artificials, it is imperative to use needle-sharp hooks. Really large pike grip baits and lures with vise-like strength, and during the hook set, the angler has to strike hard to dislodge the hook from this death grip before it can take hold in the jaw. Fishing for super-large pike is, if nothing else, physically challenging.

HOT SPOT

Manitoba

Hundreds of relatively untouched Canadian lakes, streams, and rivers hold good pike. From Labrador in the east to the far reaches of the Yukon in the northwest, Canada has incredible opportunities for anglers seeking trophy pike. With all this ground to cover, picking a specific location is difficult. However, year in and year out, more trophies come from the province of Manitoba than anywhere else. Manitoba lakes annually produce nearly 3,000 pike over the 16-pound mark. Monsters up to five feet long are caught every year, and best of all, more than 90 percent of these big fish are released alive to fight again.

Bolton Lake Lodge
Situated 300 miles north of the city of Winnipeg, Manitoba, Bolton Lake offers anglers more than 225 square miles of trophy-pike heaven. With four major river systems flowing in or out of it, it is a large, fertile system with a fascinating combination of structure types, including deep reefs, shoreline shoals, quiet back bays, surging rapids, islands, weed beds, and hundreds of channels. The main lake basin is less than 60 feet deep, allowing monster pike ready and continued access to large prey fish such as suckers, whitefish, and ciscoes.

Bolton Lake Lodge is the only outfitter on the lake. Big pike are so aggressive and plentiful that bait is not necessary. Bolton Lake Lodge is so confident anglers will catch a trophy pike that they guarantee it: if you don't boat a trophy, you stay free until you do!

Following a day of pike fighting, guests relax in modern cabins, with oil heat, electric lights, and showers.

ACCOMMODATIONS
• Two outpost cabins, two hotel rooms
• Four rooms in main lodge

MEALS
• Breakfast
• Lunch (shore lunches or packed lunches)
• Dinner
• Bar available

EQUIPMENT AVAILABLE
• 16-foot aluminum boats with swivel seats

RECOMMENDED EQUIPMENT
• Heavy-action spinning and bait-casting outfits with 20-pound-test line
• Wire leaders a must
• Top lures: T16 Kwikfish, large Rapalas, large spoons, Swim Whizz, large jigs

SEASON
• May to October
• Best fishing: May and June

CONTACT
Bolton Lake Lodge
635 Ferry Road
Winnipeg, Manitoba R3H 0T5

Peacock Bass

Scientific name: *Cichla spp.*

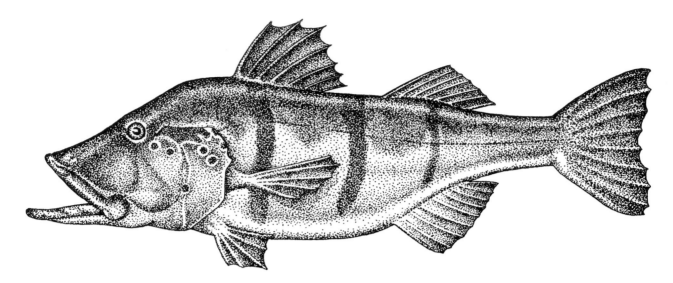

ASouth American gamefish drawing the attention of sportsmen around the world is the peacock bass. This brilliantly colored fish has even been transplanted to southern Florida. For the angler who has already sampled famous species such as bonefish, tarpon, and marlin, this freshwater fish has become one of the top-ranked new species – the "new kid on the block."

Although called a bass, the peacock, or pavón, is actually a member of the cichlid family. Besides their awesome fighting qualities, the peacock bass is aptly named for its bright coloring. There are, in fact, at least four distinct subspecies of pavón – all identical except in color pattern. Peacock bass commonly feature a dark gray/green back fading to bright gold flanks culminating in a pure white to yellowish belly. This coloration coupled with vivid dark vertically running bands or spots on the fish makes it a striking fish to behold. The spotted peacock has the same body shape, but has light, bean-sized spots arranged in two or three horizontal lines running the length of the fish. Royal peacocks, on the other hand, have yellowish bodies with darker vertical bars (not unlike a yellow perch), while butterfly peacocks have yellowish brown bodies with three or four dark blotches, edged in gold, just above the lateral line.

Orinoco River, Venezuela

Guri Lake, Venezuela

HOT SPOTS

Habitat and Behavior

Peacock bass are commonly distributed throughout the fresh waters of tropical South America. The rivers and some lakes of Venezuela, Columbia, and Brazil hold the best populations of this fish, but other tropical countries in South and Central America also host populations. Owing to the remoteness of the native territory of the peacock bass, there isn't really a whole lot known about the life of this exotic fish.

Finding the Heavyweights

The average-sized peacock weighs three to four pounds, certainly enough to satisfy even the seasoned angler. But heavyweights abound in the jungle waters. Anglers regularly hook – and lose – much larger bass.

Fishing Techniques

Finding peacock bass is relatively easy. Just look for current breaks, shoreline obstructions, rock piles, and other shallow structures. Largemouth or smallmouth bass anglers will feel quite at home when angling for peacocks. Getting the fish to hit isn't difficult either. Their frenzied attacks on schools of small fish – which look somewhat like a scene from an old movie showing piranhas gorging on the bad guy – can be quite startling. The water literally foams.

The strike of a peacock bass is mind boggling. You might at first think a transplanted 30-pound muskie had attacked your lure, only to find that you've hooked into a four-pound pavón. Indeed, the appeal of these fish is the way they strike a topwater bait. Anglers travel thousands of miles and spend thousands of dollars just to taste this experience.

Landing these fish is the real challenge. They fight so hard and will run so desperately for cover that most anglers lose their first few.

IGFA RECORD

PEACOCK BASS
Weight: 12.02 kg (26 lbs. 8 oz.)
Place: Mataveni River, Orinoco, Colombia
Date: Jan. 26, 1982
Angler: Rod Newbert, D.V.M.

Most anglers choose heavy-duty baitcasting or spinning gear for handling pavón. Pinpoint casting helps place lures in an exact location. Peacock bass, especially the big ones, tend to sit very tight to cover. The lures of

There's nothing like hooking and landing a 15-pound trophy peacock.

choice, because of the fantastic surface strikes, are noisy topwater baits like prop baits, buzzbaits, and chuggers. Subsurface minnow baits also provide great success, as do spinners and spoons. But few anglers use them, preferring instead to fish up top and enjoy the pavón's explosive surface strikes.

Flyfishing enthusiasts usually use a nine-weight outfit for peacocks, while seasoned anglers prefer to go up a notch and use a 10- or 11-weight outfit. Bushy surface flies like those one would use for pike are top choice, but flashy subsurface streamers are also highly successful.

Classic peacock-bass structure – large rock and boulders.

HOT SPOT

Guri Lake, Venezuela

Anglers who want to avoid the jungle environs can fish for peacock bass in Venezuela's Guri Lake. Deluxe accommodations can be found right on the shores of this famous 80-mile-long man-made lake, which was built by flooding valleys. Surrounding hills are carpeted with trees and dead falls. The miles of shoreline provide unlimited fishing opportunities. Catching 10 to 30 bass per day is common, and there are reports of fish in the 30-pound class. The fish population on Guri Lake is truly untapped, and most experts agree that it has world-record potential.

Guri Fishing Lodge
Located on the second-largest man-made lake in the world, Guri Fishing Lodge offers an enormous amount of prime water for peacock-bass enthusiasts. A swimming pool and a nine-hole golf course on site allow for a relaxing end to a day on the water.

ACCOMMODATIONS
• Waterfront accommodations in a comfortable inn

MEALS
• Full American Plan
• Packed shore lunch

EQUIPMENT AVAILABLE
• 18-foot fiberglass boats equipped with outboards

RECOMMENDED EQUIPMENT
• Heavy spinning or baitcasting outfits with line from 14- to 20-pound test
• Nine- or 10-weight fly outfit with plenty of backing
• Assortment of strong surface lures, spinnerbaits, jigs, spoons
• Wire leaders
• Pliers or hemostat for unhooking fish

SEASON
• Year-round
• Best fishing: winter

CONTACT
Fishing International Inc.
4010 Montecito Avenue
Santa Rosa, California
95405

HOT SPOT

Orinoco River, Venezuela

Undoubtedly the Orinoco River and its tributaries provide some of the greatest peacock bass fishing in the world. Not only can you match brute strength and brawn with the mighty peacock bass, you can also tangle with other exotic fish like piranha, the "sabre-toothed" payara, and a host of other species. This area is a jungle paradise. Monkeys, parrots, and other exotic species of animals are common. And best of all, there are no mosquitoes!

Manaka Jungle Lodge
Situated deep in the heart of the Orinoco River jungle, 420 miles south of Caracas, Manaka Jungle Lodge is the only access to an enormous section of Venezuelan jungle, including a large chunk of the Orinoco and Ventuari Rivers – both renowned peacock-bass hot spots. With gourmet meals, all the creature comforts, and an outstanding catch-and-release peacock bass fishery that's second to none, Manaka leads the way as one of the world's premiere peacock-bass destinations.

ACCOMMODATIONS
• Modern main lodge with pure water and 24-hour electricity.
• Four roomy bungalows with overhead fans and private baths.

MEALS
• Full American Plan
• Packed shore lunch

EQUIPMENT AVAILABLE
• Boats equipped with new outboards

RECOMMENDED EQUIPMENT
• Heavy spinning or baitcasting outfits with line from 14- to 20-pound test
• Nine- or 10-weight fly outfit with plenty of backing
• Assortment of strong surface lures, spinnerbaits, jigs, spoons
• Wire leaders
• Pliers or hemostat for unhooking fish

SEASON
• September to April

CONTACT
Frontiers
P.O. Box 959
Pearce Mill Road
Wexford, Pennsylvania 15090

These colorful bass love large body baits twitched just below the surface.

Smallmouth Bass

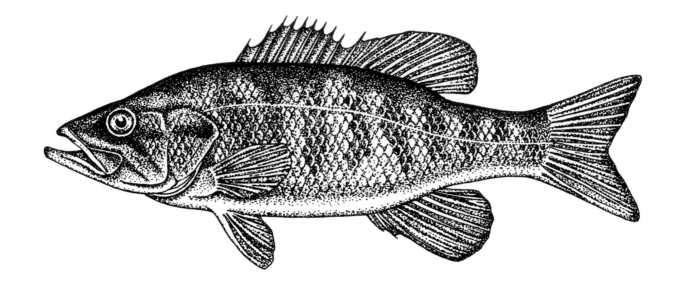

Scientific name: *Micropterus dolomieui*

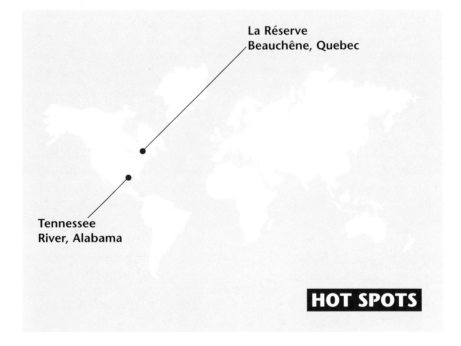

La Réserve
Beauchêne, Quebec

Tennessee
River, Alabama

HOT SPOTS

"Pound for pound, the gamest fish that swims" is the most widely repeated description of the smallmouth bass. No matter where you find them, east or west, north or south, in creeks or huge lakes, smallmouths excite anglers of all skills, ages, and abilities. Opportunistic feeders, smallmouths consume a variety of foods, from plankton and insects to frogs, crayfish, and small fish. And they do so in an aggressive style, which is just one of the reasons the smallmouth is such a popular gamefish throughout its range.

Smallmouth bass may range from brown to green with darker vertical bars along the body. They often take on a bronze color, which has earned them the nickname "bronzeback." They differ from the closely related largemouth bass in many respects. While the largemouth is a fish of shallow, weedy, warm water, smallmouth thrive in cool, rocky waters with some degree of current. Smallmouth bass can be easily differentiated from largemouths by color pattern (numerous vertical bars on the smallmouth versus a single horizontal stripe on the largemouth) and in dorsal-fin configuration (both fins are connected on the smallmouth and distinctly separated on the largemouth). Further, the smallie's lower jaw does not extend past the middle of its eye, while the largemouth's jaw extends well beyond the eye.

Habitat and Behavior

Originally, smallmouth bass were confined to waters of eastern North America, from the Great Lakes south to Alabama. Because of stocking efforts, smallmouths now are found across a large chunk of eastern North America, in scattered locations along the west coast, and even in Britain and Europe. At the

IGFA RECORD

SMALLMOUTH BASS
Weight: 5.41 kg (11 lbs. 15 oz.)
Place: Dale Hollow Lake, Kentucky, U.S.A.
Date: July 9, 1955
Angler: David L. Hayes
*(Holding fish are
Mr. and Mrs. Fetzner, donors)*

turn of the century, small-mouths were transported into new lakes via the water tanks of steam locomotives.

Smallmouth bass live strictly in fresh water, preferring clean, cool lakes and rivers. They are most active in water temperatures between 60°F and 70°F, and they try to avoid areas in excess of 74°F. They seek deeper water during the hot days of summer, returning to the shallows after water temperatures drop in the fall.

Young smallmouth bass grow rapidly at first, but their ultimate size depends on habitat conditions, the length of the growing season, water temperatures, and other factors. In the south, smallmouth bass have topped 11 pounds. However, smallmouth bass over five pounds are trophies anywhere, and bass from small rivers may be lucky to reach half that size.

Finding the Heavyweights

Canada represents the northern end of the small-mouth's range in North America. In Canada, this bass is found in Nova Scotia, New Brunswick, Quebec, Ontario, Manitoba, and British Columbia. Smallmouths have lived to a recorded age of 13 years in Canada, and have reached almost 10 pounds. The average smallie, however, weighs about one pound, and a fish of more than four pounds is a trophy.

Although smallmouth bass are aggressive and opportunistic feeders, catching the heavyweights is a matter of fishing the right places at the right time. The essential factor is water temperature. The best fishing for big smallies comes during late spring and early summer, or in the fall. In the spring you can catch large spawning fish by prowling the shallows. By fall, the big fish feed aggressively, in an effort to pack on weight before winter.

The best times to catch big smallmouths are early in the

This six-pound smallmouth beauty came out of the weeds.

HOT SPOT

Southern Ontario and Quebec

Southern Ontario and Quebec offer more lakes, ponds, and rivers with smallmouth bass than nearly all other provinces combined. Of special note are the tea-colored, wilderness waters of Rainy Lake, Namakan Lake, Lac La Croix, Sturgeon Lake, and Basswood Lake, which stretch along the border between Ontario and Minnesota; the Thousand Islands, on the St. Lawrence River; and La Réserve Beauchêne in Quebec, which offers, perhaps, the best smallmouth-bass angling in all of Canada.

La Réserve Beauchêne
La Réserve Beauchêne is a six-hour drive from Montreal, or about five hours from Toronto. The reserve offers exclusive rights to seven bass waters scattered over a vast territory. Each lake has a character all its own, but all offer a combination of shallows and deep, clear waters, with varying bottom and rocky shoreline habitat, all surrounded by picturesque scenery in an area of peace and solitude. Most waters can be reached by gravel road. Bass up to six pounds are possible. Catch-and-release is the general rule, and one reason that Beauchêne continues to produce such large bass year after year.

This reserve offers both European and American-type accommodations on some of Canada's best smallmouth bass waters. A campground is also available, providing the angler with a variety of lodging options: first class or do-it-yourself. The reserve sits just 12 miles from a paved highway on a good gravel road.

ACCOMMODATIONS
• Three camps: wood stove, kitchen or kitchenette, cold water, toilets
• Seven cottages: automatic stove, refrigerator, indoor toilet
• Main lodge

MEALS
• European plan in camps and cottages
• American Plan at main lodge
• Shore lunch/packed lunch
• BYOB

EQUIPMENT AVAILABLE
• 14- to 16-foot aluminum boats

equipped with 9.9 hp outboards
• Unlimited gas

RECOMMENDED EQUIPMENT
• Ultra-light, light- to medium-action spinning or baitcasting rods and reels
• Four- to eight-pound-test line
• Assortment of topwater and shallow running stick-baits, various spoons, buzzbaits, crankbaits, spinnerbaits, plastic worms and other plastic baits in various sizes and colors, Mepps and Blue Fox spinners, small and medium Rapalas and Rebels (floating and deep-diving), Jifterbugs, Storm "Rattlin' Thin Fin" and small and medium Flatfish
• Eight-weight fly rods
• Floating and sinking or sink-tip, weight-forward lines
• Leaders in the four- to six-pound-test range
• Muddler minnows and variations, Black/Purple Leech, various deer hair and balsa wood poppers, Dahlberg Divers, Whitlock's Mouserat, and various streamers in sizes four to eight.

SEASON
• Mid-May to mid-September
• Best trophy times: mid-June to early July and September

CONTACT
La Réserve Beauchêne
C.P. 910
Temiscamingue, Quebec
J0Z 3R0

morning and from late afternoon until just after dark.

Fishing Techniques

In the spring – when smallmouths work rocky shorelines, gravel and boulder-strewn points, and drop-offs – small spinners, shallow-running plugs, topwater baits, and streamer flies are excellent. In late spring and during the course of the summer, going deep is the general rule. Spinnerbaits, deep-running plugs, jigs, small plastic worms, and live baits (minnows, worms, leeches or crayfish) are all good. Most should be fished slowly at first, bumping the bottom, with the speed of retrieve increased if no action results. Knowing when to set the hook is critical.

Pound for pound, the smallmouth is one of the feistiest fish in fresh water.

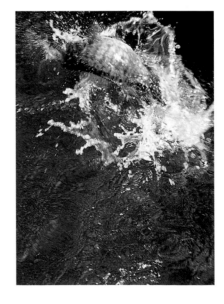

It's no wonder they call the smallmouth a "bronzeback."

On the tournament scene, landing a five-pound smallie is like landing an eight-pound largemouth.

HOT SPOT

The Deep South: Alabama

The Deep South is a place of many legends, including legendary smallmouth-bass fishing. More than four dozen major rivers, numerous creeks, nearly two dozen large reservoirs, and an unbelievable number of smaller lakes and ponds make Alabama an excellent destination for smallmouth-bass fishermen. Smallmouths grow huge in Alabama, thanks to mild winters that allow a long growing season.

One of the best spots for smallmouth bass is the 200-mile-long Tennessee River system in the north, particularly its four huge man-made reservoirs – Guntersville, Wheeler, Wilson, and Pickwick lakes. Wilson and Pickwick are top bets for genuine trophies. Smallmouths in these massive, deep, food-rich waters regularly top five and even six pounds, and seven-pound bass are always possible.

Traditional peak times are from March till early June, and again in October and November. Light baitcasting and spinning gear with lines to 10-pound test is more than adequate. Many anglers pursue these fish with ultra-light spinning or fly gear.

Smallmouths will hit just about any type and color of spinnerbait, crankbait, buzzbait, spinner, spoon, plug, and plastic worm, as long as it is relatively small. Live baits, including frogs, minnows, leeches, crayfish, and worms, are also highly effective, especially in the colder months.

Flyfishing for smallmouth is growing in popularity. A nine-foot rod designed for seven- or eight-weight line is enough to cast most smallmouth bass. Leaders should be from six- to 10-pound-test for large bass.

Motels, hotels, campgrounds, state parks with camping facilities and cabins, as well as boats, guides, bait and tackle are available on or near each lake. For further information on fishing in Alabama, contact

Alabama Game & Fish Division
64 N. Union Street
Room 551
Montgomery, Alabama
36130

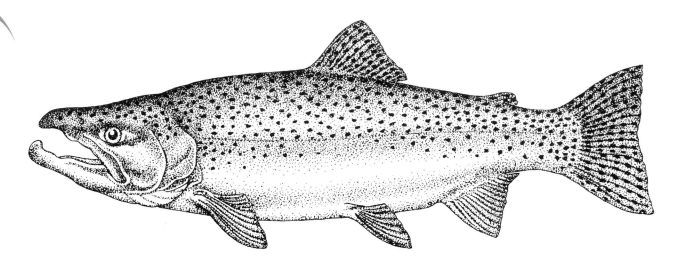

Steelhead (Rainbow)

Scientific name: *Oncorhynchus mykiss*

Widely transplanted outside its original range in western North America, the rainbow trout has become firmly established throughout most of North America and in parts of Britain, Europe, Asia, Australia, New Zealand, and South America. One of the most adaptable of the salmonoids, the rainbow trout today is found in lakes, rivers, streams, and ponds throughout much of the world. Anadromous populations, which migrate to and from the sea or large inland lakes, also exist in many areas and carry the resonant name "steelhead." The anadromous population consistently gains the greatest size, so for our purposes we will discuss primarily the "steelhead" variation of the rainbow trout.

The rainbow is famed for its fighting power, its high, twisting leaps, and its stamina. It always puts up a good fight, and landing one from a small, brushy stream can be quite an accomplishment. In large rivers or lakes, where they have plenty of room to move about, the steelhead variation has been known to leap more than four feet out of the water when hooked. Large migratory steelhead also have been known to leap dams and waterfalls more than 10 feet high.

Steelhead are quite adaptable for a trout species, thriving in all sorts of waters. As a result, they can display an enormous variation in coloration and shape from place to place. Lake-dwelling rainbows often feature deep, thick bodies with relatively small heads and fins, with dark blue, green, or black backs peppered with black dots, silvery sides, and white undersides. Stream-dwelling fish are often highly marked, with green, blue, or brown backs and brilliant flanks cloaked in iridescent green, blue, purple, pink, and silver, often with pink or blazing

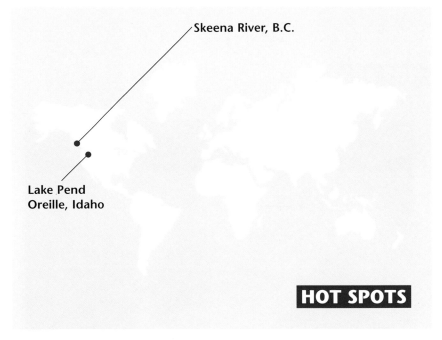

Skeena River, B.C.

Lake Pend Oreille, Idaho

HOT SPOTS

IGFA RECORD

STEELHEAD TROUT

Weight: 19.10 kg (42 lbs. 2 oz.)
Place: Bell Island, Alaska, U.S.A
Date: June 22, 1970
Angler: David Robert White
(representative size shown)

red gill covers. These stream fish are normally heavily covered in small black spots. Anadromous fish normally assume the silvery coloration of their lake cousins, but retain the long, slim body shape of stream fish. In areas where rainbow trout from a variety of geographic areas have been introduced, it is sometimes possible to catch several fish over the course of a day that all look somewhat different.

Habitat and Behavior

Steelhead have strong migratory instincts, and whenever possible, they will migrate downstream into large lakes or the ocean. The fish grow fast in the big water, then return to the parent stream to spawn. Normally this migration takes place in the early spring, but some fish may return to their parent river several months in advance. Most steelhead spawn in the spring when the water temperature reaches just above 50°F.

In big water, steelhead relate to the surface and are pelagic, wandering widely in small, loose schools, usually near concentrations of small prey fish. They respond well to trolled lures, particularly silver and blue spoons.

Finding the Heavyweights

Rainbow trout vary widely in size, depending on their habitat. Fish from small streams, ponds, or small mountain lakes may average one pound or less, and any trout over two or three pounds could be considered a trophy. On the other hand, migratory rainbows from the Great Lakes or large impoundments regularly top 10 pounds and may exceed 20. Ocean-run steelhead

An impressive winter rainbow from the Niagara River.

HOT SPOT

Lake Pend Oreille, Idaho

World-famous Lake Pend Oreille, in the state of Idaho, inevitably comes up in any talk about trophy rainbow trout. Most of Pend Oreille's big rainbows are caught by trolling late in the season (October or November) with large plugs. Oddly, one of the main forage fish in the lake is smaller rainbow trout. Lures that imitate the color pattern of an immature trout produce best.

Because fishing is big business at Pend Oreille, guides and accommodations are readily available in the nearby hamlet of Sand Point. For information on guides and outfitters, contact

CONTACT
Idaho Guides and Outfitters
Association
Box 95
Boise, Idaho 83701

grow even larger, and have been known to exceed 40 pounds.

Fishing Techniques

Steelhead attack a variety of natural baits, artificial lures, and flies, plus an assortment of somewhat unusual baits, including cheese, corn, miniature marshmallows, and even raspberries. There isn't much a rainbow trout won't eat, a fact that makes it a popular and generally cooperative gamefish across its range.

Steelhead are hardly shy, and larger ones can be quite aggressive, eagerly tackling even large prey items. In large bodies of water, where the trout feed most heavily on smaller fish, anglers troll or cast fish-imitating lures like spoons, minnow plugs, or long crankbaits. Fly rodders usually give the nod to large, bright streamers such as the Micky Finn.

Steelhead in a river environment are approached differently. The steelhead's Achilles' heel is its penchant for snacking on roe, including trout and salmon eggs. It's not uncommon to catch steelhead or rainbow with their digestive tracts absolutely stuffed with golden eggs. Small clumps of roe and its imitations are therefore the number-one bait for rainbow trout in rivers. Depending on the season, water color, and size of the river, anglers fish roe in sizes anywhere from one tiny salmon egg up to a clump of roe the size of a golf ball. The bait is drifted either directly on bottom, or suspended beneath a suitably sized float. Steelhead usually sit close to, or right on, the stream bed, so presenting your bait at the fish's level is essential.

Tackle is selected to match the stream. In small, open rivers, relatively light, long spinning outfits and six- or eight-pound-test line work well. In larger flows, long salmon rods, high capacity levelwind reels and line from 12- to 20-pound-test make more sense. Hooked steelhead normally make repeated long, powerful runs either with or against the current, interspersed with several high, twisting jumps. Holding on to one in an obstruction-filled river with a powerful current can prove exceptionally challenging, even for experienced anglers.

Some of the best steelhead waters can be reached only by helicopter.

The Lake Ontario watershed contains many small rivers and streams that have major steelhead runs.

HOT SPOT

Skeena River, British Columbia

For the angler seeking the very biggest rainbow trout, British Columbia's massive Skeena River system can't be beaten. The river and its major tributaries host a strong run of massive sea-run rainbows each year, including numerous fish over 20 pounds. The best shot at a huge fish comes in the spring from March till May.

The Skeena's reputation as a top location for trophy rainbows has launched a substantial tourism industry in the area. Guides and lodging are readily available.

Eagle Lodge

Situated just north of the scenic village of Terrace, near the Kalum River, the lodge is operated by Northwest Fishing Guides, who have exclusive access to some of the finest salmon and steelhead water in British Columbia. With all modern conveniences and warm hospitality, this lodge is a fully equipped fishing camp.

ACCOMMODATIONS
• Main lodge
• Dining lodge
• Games room
• Access to hot springs

MEALS
• Breakfast
• Packed lunch or shore lunch
• Dinner
• BYOB, but offers an honor bar

EQUIPMENT AVAILABLE
• Drift boats and jet boats
• Helicopter excursions
• Spinning and trolling tackle

RECOMMENDED EQUIPMENT
• Medium- or heavy-weight fly rods with double handle, reels with good drags, nine- to 10-weight sinking line.
• leaders 12- to 17-pound test
• streamers or roe imitations

If spinning:
• Medium- or medium-heavy-action rods six to seven feet
• Baitcasting or spinning reels, 10- to 17-pound test; wire leader; spoons, like the Pixie (use single hooks); feathered or curly-tail jigs in bright colors

SEASON
• July–September
• Best fishing: August

CONTACT
Northwest Fishing Guides
P.O. Box 434
Terrace, British Columbia V8G 4B1

Top left: This hefty female took a single egg with light line and a float reel. *Bottom left:* Sometimes it takes the right fly and a perfect presentation to hook a 20-pounder. *Right:* A beautiful British Columbia steelhead is taken on a fly.

Striped Bass

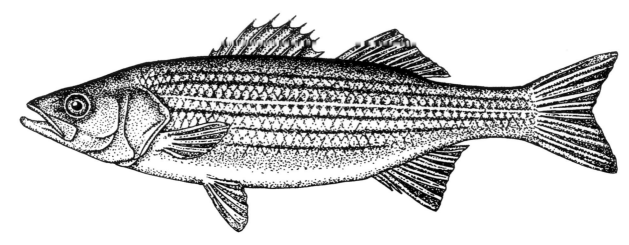

Scientific name: *Morone saxatilis*

For anglers who surf-cast along North America's beaches, drift with the tide along inshore reefs, or probe the depths of large, freshwater impoundments, the striped bass is king. This large, aggressive bass lives along both coasts of North America and has been introduced to numerous reservoirs in the eastern and southern United States. In many cases, it has flourished to the point that intensive recreational fisheries have resulted.

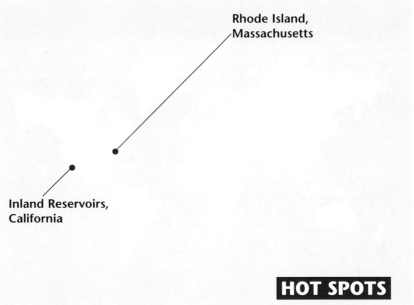

Rhode Island, Massachusetts

Inland Reservoirs, California

HOT SPOTS

Habitat and Behavior

The striper is a coastal fish, seldom found far from shore. An important commercial species throughout its range, it fetches a hefty price in most fish stores. Native to the Atlantic coast of North America from Canada's Maritime provinces to northern Florida, it was introduced to the Pacific coast off California in the late 1800s and today thrives from southern California to the Columbia River. The San Francisco Bay area boasts an outstanding population of striped bass.

Striped bass lead varied lifestyles. Some bass adopt a nomadic lifestyle and migrate the entire length of the Atlantic coast; others live their entire lives in a single bay or river estuary. Anyone interested in catching striped bass would be wise to hire a good fishing guide or, at the least, consult local tackle stores or game and fish departments.

Most saltwater bass migrate each fall to their spawning sites, usually at the lower end of a large river. Some may spend the winter in brackish or fresh water before heading upriver to spawn in May or June. Females lay anywhere from a few thousand to more than three million eggs. Although female stripers can spawn several times during their lifetime, they don't necessarily spawn each year. Mortality of young stripers is high. Adult striped bass weigh anywhere from five to 20 pounds, though fish topping 50 pounds show up now and then.

To reach these sizes, striped bass gorge on small schooling fish, such as herring, menhaden, alewives, silversides, and shad. In addition, they also eat marine worms, and crustaceans (including lobster).

Finding the Heavyweights

With a maximum weight in excess of 70 pounds, striped bass are among the largest fish available to surf anglers in North America. Although the Pacific coast produces very large stripers, the majority of record fish come from the eastern seaboard of the United States, with New Jersey, Massachusetts, New York, and Connecticut leading the way.

Few freshwater stripers reach the massive size of ocean fish, but numerous bass up to 60 pounds come from impoundments in California and Tennessee. Although these freshwater reservoirs still can't match the oceans when it comes to ultimate size, they are certainly capable of producing very big fish.

Fishing Techniques

Since stripers often feed on the surface, poppers and light

IGFA RECORD

STRIPED BASS
Weight: 35.60 kg (78 lbs. 8 oz.)
Place: Atlantic City, N.J., U.S.A.
Date: Sept. 21, 1982
Angler: Albert R. McReynolds

Many of the trophy stripers can be caught from shore.

HOT SPOT

Rhode Island

Each fall, in the first hazy light of morning, there is an ominous quality to the shorelines of Westerly, Rhode Island. Under a pastel sky, lone striper diehards gather for those precious minutes when large fish are on the feed. Drifting with the current, eyes glued on the surface where their baitfish swim, they anxiously monitor the free-spooling line with their thumbs, waiting for the sign – that first splash of a menhaden leaping from the water to avoid its assailant. A striper will sometimes chase a prey for more than a minute, even thrashing it with its tail before swallowing it headfirst. When the angler thinks the bait has been swallowed, he or she clicks on the brake, watches the line tighten, and heaves back on the rod. Inevitably, the angler becomes hooked into the emotion that bass hunters commonly call stripermania.

There are plenty of reasons to fall for stripermania in Rhode Island. Striper fishing there is a generations-old tradition, one that centers on big fish. Double-digit-weight bass are common catches.

Asking at local bait and tackle shops should reveal two or three good prospects. A quick scouting trip then tells you all you need to know. If you spot other anglers, chances are the fish are on. Striper fishing is an all-year affair, with the months of July, August, and March producing the majority of big fish. For information on fishing and accommodations, contact

Rhode Island Division of
Fish & Wildlife
Stedman Government Center
Tower Hill Road
Wakefield, Rhode Island 02879

spoons like the Hopkins or Arbogast Doctor Spoons are effective. When surf-casting, long, powerful spinning or baitcasting rods are needed to cast far enough to reach the fish. Most anglers go with 15- to 20-pound monofilament. During the summer months, landlocked stripers often avoid warm waters by entering a tributary river or stream, where short rods and heavy line are necessary for snag-infested settings.

Fishing at dawn and dusk is most productive when water temperatures begin to rise. Whereas young schooling stripers can tolerate temperatures of up to 80°F, the large adults avoid water over 72°F. Not only are the twilight hours cooler, but they are also the time when surface waters are most calm, making it easier to corral baitfish.

In lakes and reservoirs, care should be taken not to spook or scatter a school of feeding fish by casting in the middle of them. A more effective approach is to follow the school with an electric motor and cast toward the outer perimeter of the school.

The most obvious sign of stripers is bird activity overhead. Surf casters will often wait along beaches or reefs for the first signs of gulls or baitfish breaking the surface, often during an incoming or outgoing tide. In fresh water, finding structures such as underwater humps, ledges, points, narrows, and back ends of coves pays best. Troll these areas with spoons or crankbaits to find fish.

Stiped bass can be quite finicky, refusing artificial presentations. Instead, try drifting with the wind or using an electric motor, rigging a live gizzard shad, alewife, or even a panfish and allowing it to swim freely behind the boat. The use of extra weight or leader should be avoided, if possible. Stripers do not have sharp enough teeth to cut line, but be warned – in salt water, razor-toothed bluefish often nab baits and lures intended for stripers.

The choice of bait should depend on what is locally available. For example, in the fall, east-coast anglers prefer menhaden, which are then abundant as they migrate toward their spawning rivers. Although they are an extremely difficult fish to keep alive, in season they outproduce any other offering. In May and June, young eels become the main menu, and twitching them along the bottom, usually with a slightly weighted jig head, yields excellent results.

When casting lures at fish feeding below the surface, many anglers like to improve their odds by using a surgeon rig to splice a leader and jig above the spoon. Others use a three-way swivel about two feet above the spoon and attach a short dropper line with about one-half ounce of lead. Dead bait or bunker (usually dead menhaden) is the most common bait, especially at night. Rigging cels at night is also common practice. Eels are nocturnal by nature, and in warm water, bass will frequently hunt them by moonlight.

HOT SPOT

California

Though California's massive inland reservoirs may not produce bass in the 70-pound class, they do harbor huge numbers of very big stripers. Some anglers suggest the next all-tackle record striped bass may well be a freshwater fish from California.

Because the state's bass reservoirs are spread over a broad area, the level of accommodations and services varies widely. First-time anglers are advised to hire a guide, at least for the first day of their trip. Monster striped bass are a possibility at any time, but April, May, and June are the most consistent months for the big ones.

For further information about fishing California's freshwater reservoirs for monster stripers, contact

California Department
of Fish & Game
1416 Ninth Street
Sacramento, California 95814

Walleye

Scientific name: *Stizostedion vitreum vitreum*

The walleye has long been considered one of the most popular gamefish in North America, even though it is not difficult to find or to catch. Even big walleyes are somewhat less than inspired fighters, far better known for their qualities on the dinner plate.

Yet even though they may not break rods and lines, walleye are still just plain fun to catch, and they have a near-fanatical following across North America. So great is the walleye's popularity that professional walleye tournaments now rival professional bass tournaments for the interest generated and amount of prize money awarded annually. One can now find specialized walleye tackle, walleye magazines, walleye clubs, and even walleye boats just about anywhere in North America.

The North American midwest, even with its great population density and resulting fishing pressure, still provides the greatest walleye

Bay of Quinte, Ontario

Saginaw Bay, Michigan

HOT SPOTS

fishery in the world. It is here that single huge fish don't count as much as stringers of average-sized fish. Anglers tell tales of stringers of eight-pounders. Now that's the stuff of true legends.

The walleye has a rounded, elongated body with greenish to bright yellow flanks framed with a dark back and a sometimes pure white belly. The characteristic that gives it its name is

the large, prominent, glassy white eye. The walleye has several very sharp teeth along with a large spiny dorsal fin.

Habitat and Behavior

The walleye is found throughout much of the fresh waters of North America. In Canada it ranges from Quebec in the east to British Columbia and the Yukon in the west, and as far north as the Mackenzie River Delta. Although it is native to most of the northern U.S., stocking has expanded its distribution dramatically, and today walleyes can be found from coast to coast, north to south.

Walleyes are a cool-water fish. They often occupy large lakes and river systems in medium depth ranges. They are seldom found in water with temperatures considered comfortable for largemouth bass, but will associate more closely with the habitat and temperatures usually reserved for smallmouths.

Rocky drop-offs, points, sand flats, and deep weed beds are all considered prime walleye habitat. They are usually structure oriented, but in larger lakes, such as the Great Lakes, they frequently adopt a pelagic lifestyle and suspend in open water near schools of smaller baitfish.

Finding the Heavyweights

The biggest walleyes come from the central United States impoundments, but

IGFA RECORD

WALLEYE
Weight: 11.34 kg (25 lbs.)
Place: Old Hickory Lake, Tennessee, U.S.A.
Date: Aug. 1, 1960
Angler: Mabry Harper

Many river systems in North America produce hefty walleye.

HOT SPOT

Saginaw Bay, Michigan

Without question, the nearest rival to Ontario's Bay of Quinte as a trophy walleye hot spot is Michigan's Saginaw Bay, on the western shoreline of Lake Huron. This waterway produces incredible numbers of big walleyes, including double-digit-weight fish. While nearby Lake Erie may produce more five- to eight-pound fish, it can't hold a candle to the ability of Saginaw Bay to produce genuine lunkers.

Fishing Saginaw Bay for the first time is simple. Just look for other boats. Saginaw is one of those spots where you won't lack company. Happily, local anglers don't mind sharing tips, since most realize there are plenty of big fish to go round. Checking in at shoreline bait shops is the fastest way to obtain up-to-date information.

Hotels, motels, and campgrounds are available in nearby Bay City.

Full-meal packages are often available with accommodations, and a range of restaurants is found in Bay City and surrounding area.

RECOMMENDED EQUIPMENT
• Large, seaworthy walleye-style boat with outboard
• Medium-fast spinning outfit suitable for jigging with eight-pound-test-line
• Long, light-medium spinning outfit for crankbaiting
• Heavy spinning or baitcasting rod for trolling
• Planer boards
• Diving planers
• Selection of in-line spinners, weight-forward spinners, jigs and crankbaits
• Live-bait rigs

SEASON
• All year long
• Best fishing: October and November

CONTACT
Michigan Travel Bureau
P.O. Box 3393
Livonia, Michigan
48151

the most recent walleye hot spot to gain prominence is the Great Lakes. Ontario's Bay of Quinte boasts a phenomenal fishery where 10-pound walleyes don't even raise an eyebrow, and fish to 18 pounds turn up each year. Other hot spots include the eastern end of Lake Ontario, the whole of Lake Erie, and the Saginaw Bay and Little Bay de Noc areas of Lake Huron. While those southern reservoirs may indeed produce massive walleyes, they can't compare to the big lakes when it comes to sheer numbers of 10-pound-plus fish. Any walleye over 10 pounds is a true trophy.

Fishing Techniques

Techniques and tactics for catching big walleyes fall in two basic categories: trolling and jigging. In most walleye lakes and rivers, the fish feed and locate adjacent to bottom structure or deep weed beds. Jigs with soft plastic twister tails, buck tails, or other dressings are probably the most popular style of baits. Colors vary, but favorites tend to be yellow or chartreuse, along with black or white. Many anglers will add worms, leeches, or minnows to these lures to tempt particularly fussy fish.

Trolling ranks as the second most popular walleye technique. Indeed, walleye trolling has evolved into an art form, with anglers continually honing their presentations in response to prevalent conditions. One prime example would be the development of backtrolling. Successful anglers have discovered that boat (and therefore lure) control is greatly enhanced by trolling backward – driving the boat stern-first. This method allows a lure or bait to be precisely positioned so that an angler can follow a weed line, drop-off, or other structural break. Special walleye boats have been developed with "splash" guards on the transom to help withstand the spray and wash from trolling backward in open waters on windy days.

Downrigging also plays an important part in catching suspended walleye in large, open waters such as the Great Lakes, especially Lake Erie. Here the fish roam widely in pursuit of schools of forage fish. Because these fish may be 70 feet down and stacked into a narrow band of water perhaps no more than five feet thick, downrigging – which allows anglers to troll at exact depths with even light tackle – is the tactic of choice. Anglers will run a variety of body baits and spoons to catch some impressive numbers and sizes of fish. Surface planers with body baits will also produce some quality fish

Two for the table and one 17-pound trophy for the wall.

HOT SPOT

Bay of Quinte, Ontario

The Bay of Quinte is a large bay located on the northern shore of Lake Ontario near the cities of Belleville and Trenton, Ontario. It is the site for one of the most phenomenal walleye ice fisheries in North America. When ice first forms around Christmas, anglers by the hundreds descend on the Bay of Quinte. They customarily use a variety of jigging spoons tipped with three- to six-inch live minnows. Huge fish are commonly caught through the winter months and 10-pounders are not unusual. And every year someone lays claim to a 17-pound-plus fish.

Quinte offers hot walleye action year-round, except in the warm months, when the biggest fish abandon the bay for the deeper, cooler waters of Lake Ontario proper.

Most visiting anglers fish from their own boats and stay in motels. Launching facilities are located in most shoreline towns.

RECOMMENDED EQUIPMENT
• Walleye-style boat with outboard and electric motor
• Light jigging rod with eight- to 12-pound-test line
• Heavy crankbait outfit
• Medium spinning outfit for live bait
• Assortment of jigs, crankbaits and live-bait rigs

SEASON
• May to March
• Best fishing: November
• Ice fishing: December to March

CONTACT
Tourism Ontario
77 Bloor Street West, 9th Floor
Toronto, Ontario M7A 2R9

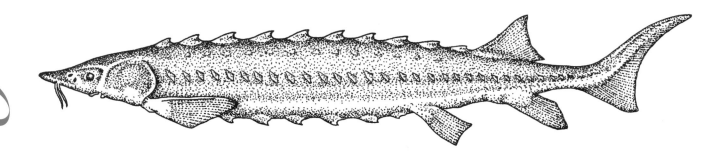

White Sturgeon

Scientific name: *Acipenser transmontanus*

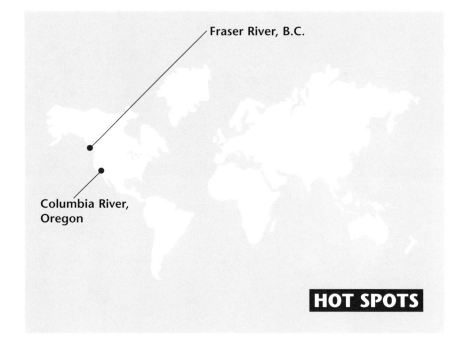

Fraser River, B.C.

Columbia River, Oregon

HOT SPOTS

There are several species of sturgeon worldwide, but the most sought after is the mighty white. Capable of reaching weights in excess of 400 pounds, these enormous fish put up spectacular battles, often clearing the water when hooked, offering a unique brand of freshwater big-game fishing.

Throughout the west coast of North America, both bank and boat fishermen can be found all season long, casting a variety of baits with ultra-heavy gear, hoping to catch these prehistoric-looking bottom feeders. Tales of gigantic sturgeon weighing anywhere from 1,000 to 2,000 pounds are numerous, as are tales of mighty fish so huge that they hauled anglers, horses, and even tractors into the water in the course of the fight. Supporting these wild tales are old photographs showing huge sturgeon up to 10 feet long. By the early 1900s, the white sturgeon were almost

brought to extinction because of senseless slaughter and by commercial over-harvesting, primarily for caviar. Many early commercial salmon fishermen considered them a nuisance because they became entangled in nets. At one time it was common procedure to simply cut off their tails and then let them go. More recently, pollution and hydroelectric developments have affected sturgeon runs.

However, management programs created to protect this magnificent fish have began to show positive results.

The white sturgeon's pointed snout, elongated shark-like body, basket-shaped sucker mouth, bony protective plates, and sheer size make it virtually impossible to mistake it for any other type of freshwater fish. Sturgeon have small eyes and relatively poor vision. They use their keen sense of smell and four facial barbells to forage along the bottom.

Habitat and Behavior

The white sturgeon leads an anadromous life, much like that of a salmon, in that it spawns in fresh water but spends most of its life in the sea. The white sturgeon can be found along most of the Pacific coast of North America, from California north to the Aleutian Islands of Alaska. Very little is known about its life cycle or habits, and it is very rarely caught – or even seen – in salt water. The lone exception is San Francisco Bay, where an intensive saltwater sturgeon fishery exists. Otherwise, virtually all white-sturgeon fishing takes place in the lower section of its freshwater spawning rivers. Intense sturgeon fisheries exist on most major west coast rivers, including the massive Columbia and Fraser systems.

Young adults spawn about once every four years, but as they grow older, sturgeon spawn only once every decade or so. Spawning usually takes place in May or June in river rapids, below waterfalls, or in deep rocky pools with a strong current. It is believed that most large sturgeon enter their spawning rivers in early spring, returning to salt water after spawning in mid- to late summer. Some have been known to overwinter in the lower stretches of a river. Landlocked populations of white sturgeon exist in some areas. These fish may be mistaken by anglers for the smaller and more common lake sturgeon.

The food of white sturgeon includes a variety of

IGFA RECORD

STURGEON, WHITE
Weight: 212.28 kg (468 lbs.)
Place: Benicia, California, U.S.A.
Date: July 9, 1983
Angler: Joey Pallotta III

This is the largest type of fish found in the inland waters of the United States.

HOT SPOT

Columbia River, Oregon

The world-famous Columbia River has miles of sturgeon water available to anglers. Among the most notable stretches is the Dodson area, situated near Portland, Oregon. It extends from Rooster Rock to the Bonneville Dam on Bradford Island and can be reached from the town of Covert's Landing.

When you're waiting for the big one to strike, a helpful precaution consists of attaching a buoy to the anchor line. In fast current, such as below the Bonneville Dam, you may need to chase a fish in a hurry without losing the anchor. Better yet, hire a guide so you can relax and concentrate on fishing!

For information on fishing the Columbia sturgeon run, contact

The Fishery
HC66, Box 432
Cascade Locks, Oregon
97014

excellent shot at tangling with a trophy. This massive waterway has produced some enormous fish. Archival records document sturgeon up to 1,800 pounds taken near the town of Mission, and a magnificent 1,387 pounder taken near New Westminster in 1897. Although the majority of sturgeon caught today weigh from 60 to 300 pounds, the possibility of hooking an old grandfather pushing or perhaps exceeding 1,000 pounds keeps anglers coming back year after year.

Two basic methods are used to catch white sturgeon.

Fishing from the shore of a fast-moving river for white sturgeon is a bit like taking Huck Finn's catfish tactics to a new level, with the cane pole replaced by a sturdy, saltwater outfit and 40-pound-test line. Often the anglers will clip a small bell to the rod tip, to warn of a sturgeon hit (particularly when fishing at night). The terminal rig, meanwhile, resembles the walleye angler's three-way swivel arrangement, but also on a grand scale, with the small lead weight replaced with a railroad spike hefty enough to hold the bait in place in the current. An 18-inch leader of 50- to 80-pound test is then tied on with a strong number four or six single hook. Sturgeon do not have any sharp teeth in their leathery mouths, but sharp, bony plates on their bodies can weaken or slice the leader if the fish rolls on it.

The approach used by

dead fish and animals (they particularly love lampreys), although small live fish can easily be vacuumed into their voluminous mouths. Sticklebacks, sculpins, eulachon, smelt, and even shad or salmon carcasses contribute to the sturgeon's diet.

Sturgeon live remarkably long lives, but they grow very slowly. The largest specimens caught were most probably well over a century old.

Finding the Heavyweights

The Oregon Historical Society possesses several genuinely shocking photos of leviathans, such as a 1,500-pounder from the Snake River near Payette, Idaho. Today, such sizable fish seem impossible, at least in North American waters, and any fish over 250 pounds should be considered an honest trophy.

Fishing Techniques

British Columbia, on Canada's west coast, is the place to be for big sturgeon today. The Fraser River system, including the Harrison, Stellako, and lower Pitt rivers, offers anglers an boat anglers isn't much different, although the dropper line is usually replaced with a sliding sinker rig, using a pyramid weight in calm water and a very heavy ball sinker when fishing strong currents. Sometimes it is necessary to add up to 48 ounces of lead in very swift water. Just thinking about fishing with a weight of this size puts the sturgeon's power into a tangible perspective.

Boat anglers tend to take a more active approach to sturgeon fishing than do bank fishermen. They slowly "walk" the bait downstream with the current, allowing a more natural presentation than afforded by a bait simply anchored on bottom. Where legal, adult sea lampreys are the bait of choice.

Expert sturgeon anglers claim the stinkiest, oiliest baits work best. In fact some anglers go as far as to "spice up" their baits with a variety of substances, including the oils, extracts, and even parts of a variety of dead critters.

Although sturgeon are not necessarily considered nocturnal feeders, most sturgeon anglers and fishing guides claim to have the best results on overnight excursions.

As a rule, bank rods are longer than boat rods, but both should be of the heavy-action variety. An 11-footer is appropriate for long casts from shore, but in a boat a shorter six-to seven-footer is easier to handle. These are usually matched to very high-quality, high-capacity level-wind reels with top-notch star drags.

HOT SPOT

Fraser River, British Columbia

Situated many miles upstream from the Fraser's delta and the city of Vancouver, the village of Mission offers anglers perhaps the best opportunity to catch large white sturgeon anywhere. At night, when the river's traffic has subsided and the tug boats have retired, only a few silhouettes remain anchored strategically next to a slough near a sand bank, or at the mouth of the Vedder River (a tributary to the Fraser). All is quiet except for the occasional splash of a 20-ounce lead sinker, and the murmur of voices, which halt every time there's a ring from one of the small tin bells clipped to the rod tips. Usually it's just the wind, but sometimes . . .

In August, when skies are clear, anglers may witness dazzling displays of northern lights and the occasional shooting star, as the eerie sound of an incoming train echoes through the mountains. In the morning, it is common for a fog to roll in and bathe the valley in soft shades of pastel blue or crimson. This magnificent panorama makes a fitting backdrop for some of the world's most exciting fresh water big-game fishing. For information on Fraser River white sturgeon action, contact

Sportfishing Travel Network
937 Centre Road,
Dept 2020
Waterdown, Ontario
L0R 2H0

Saltwater Fish

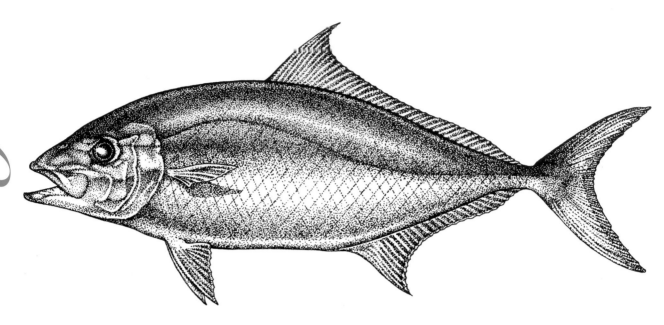

Greater Amberjack

Scientific name: *Seriola dumerili*

Pound for pound, the greater amberjack is one of the toughest opponents available to saltwater fishermen. It has a well-justified reputation for testing angler and tackle alike, with many encounters resulting in victory for the fish.

Amberjacks bear a superficial resemblance to bluefish in general body shape, but they lack the bluefish's sharp, prominent teeth. In fact, amberjacks are much closer in overall appearance and coloration to the Californian and southern yellowtails of the Pacific. The greater amberjack can be distinguished from these closely related species by gill-raker and fin-ray counts. Generally speaking, amberjacks are also more heavily built and deeper bodied than yellowtail of a similar length.

On most live or freshly caught amberjacks, a dark diagonal stripe runs from the mouth area up through the eye toward the first dorsal fin, and a broad, amber-colored lateral stripe runs horizontally along the fish's flanks. These stripes often intensify when the amberjack is hooked or actively feeding, but may fade rapidly after death.

Habitat and Behavior

Amberjacks are found throughout the temperate and tropical seas of the world, including the Indo-Pacific region around southern Japan, parts of China, the Philippines, and Australia, and in the central Pacific, particularly off Hawaii. In addition, they occur throughout the warmer portions of the western Atlantic Ocean, as well as parts of the eastern Atlantic, from Madeira to southwest Africa. Amberjacks are also found sporadically in warmer

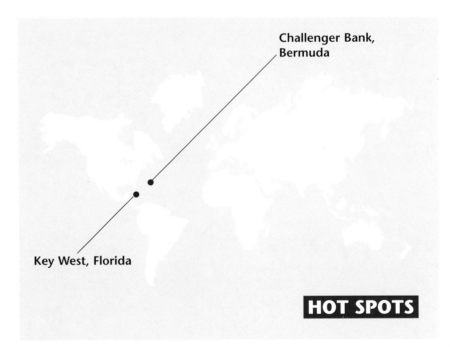

Challenger Bank, Bermuda

Key West, Florida

HOT SPOTS

The amberjack is a slick and muscular fish, which makes it a prize catch for any angler.

IGFA RECORD

GREATER AMBERJACK
Weight: 70.59 kg (155 lbs. 10 oz.)
Place: Challenger Bank, Bermuda
Date: June 24, 1981
Angler: Joseph Dawson

sections of the Mediterranean Sea. In the western Atlantic, amberjacks are most abundant around the Bahamas, Bermuda, Cuba, and southern Florida, but will sometimes range northward along the Atlantic seaboard as far as the Carolinas and Virginia, particularly in late summer and early fall when the water is warmest. Amberjacks swim mainly near the surface layers in warm, clean, open waters, but can also be caught at considerable depths over reefs, wrecks, and sea mounts, as well as around offshore islands, buoys, oil rigs, piers, and the like.

A schooling, structure-loving species, amberjacks prey upon a broad range of marine fish, including runners, scad, smaller jacks, grunts, chubs, and various reef fish, as well as squid, octopus, crabs, and shrimp. They are aggressive, competitive hunters and, once they reach larger sizes, have few natural enemies apart from sharks and large billfish. As a result, big amberjacks tend to be inquisitive and fearless, often swimming right up to boats, particularly when other fish are being hooked, played, or landed.

Finding the Heavyweights

The greater amberjack is the largest of all the jack species, growing to as much as 160

HOT SPOT

Challenger Bank, Bermuda

The Challenger Bank off Bermuda is a prime destination for anglers seeking big amberjacks. Budding record hunters would be well advised to gear up with sturdy tackle when pursuing Challenger's giant jacks, despite the fact that 100-pound-plus specimens have been taken here in the past on lines as light as 20-pound test.

The prime months for catching big amberjacks on Challenger Bank are June and July. Live baits are the preferred offering, although some fish also fall to trolled or cast lures.

Lodges and fishing guides are readily available in Bermuda. For specific information, contact

Sportfishing Travel Network
937 Centre Road
Waterdown, Ontario L0R 2H0

pounds on rare occasion.

The famed Challenger Bank, off the Atlantic island of Bermuda, is one of the best places in the world to search for a record-breaking greater amberjack. This area may not offer the quantities of amberjack sometimes found in places such as Key West or Bimini, but what Bermuda's jacks lack in numbers, they more than make up for in sheer size.

HOT SPOT

Key West, Florida

If Bermuda is the place to chase an all-tackle amberjack record, then Key West, at the southern tip of Florida, is certainly the number-one destination for light- and medium-tackle anglers. Here, the best action typically occurs over sunken wrecks, reef pinnacles, and around artificial structures such as navigation markers and buoys, with the peak action coming from December to April. Fish to 30 pounds are relatively common off Key West, with the occasional fish to 100 pounds or more.

Key West guides and skippers are particularly adept at chumming and teasing amberjacks to the surface for fly casters and ultra-light fans.

Lodges and fishing guides are almost everywhere in the fabled Florida Keys. For detailed information, contact

Florida Department of Commerce
Room 505, Collins Building
107 W. Gaines
Tallahassee, Florida
32399-2000

Heavy concentrations can be found around reefs, wrecks, and buoys.

The amberjack strikes fast, fights hard, and often tries to hold bottom.

Fishing Techniques

Amberjacks are keenly sought by many saltwater fishers because of their sporting qualities. They strike hard, fight strongly, and frequently dive for the sea bed, sometimes slicing the angler's line on reef outcrops, mooring cables, or other debris. When one amberjack is brought to the boat, others in the school

Left: The proper fishing gear makes landing the big one an easier task.

will often follow the hooked fish to the surface.

Fishing methods include trolling near the surface with various skirted lures, spoons, plugs, jigs, or strip baits. Amberjacks are also caught while fishing with live mullet, grunts, pinfish, or other small baitfish, and many incidental catches of amberjacks are made while bottom-fishing for snappers and groupers with cut baits and jigs.

Anglers attract aggressive fish by chumming with fish scraps, or teasing them to the surface with hookless lures

or tethered live baits. At that point they can be easily hooked with light casting tackle or fly rods.

Although small- to medium-sized amberjacks have white, tasty flesh, the greater amberjack is high on the list of 300 or more species of tropical marine fish suspected of occasionally causing ciguatera poisoning. For this reason alone, amberjacks should be released unless specifically intended for wall-mounting or weighing-in for record claims.

Great Barracuda

Scientific name: *Sphyraena barracuda*

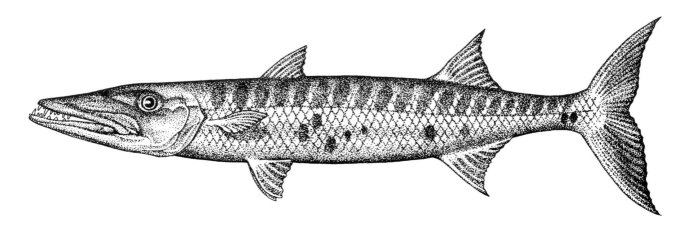

The famous and fabled barracuda, or 'cuda for short, is a powerful, toothy, opportunistic predator, eating whatever is available and often attacking quite large prey. This quality, combined with the 'cuda's wild antics on the end of a line, make it a first-class sportfish.

Sometimes called the wolf of the sea, the barracuda has a fearsome and much exaggerated reputation that is greatly enhanced by its malevolent look and large, sharp teeth. Barracudas are credited with savage attacks upon humans, although there is little documentation to authenticate most of these claims.

Large barracudas do frequently follow divers, giving more than one a bad scare. Nevertheless, even very large barracudas do not usually attack divers unless first speared or provoked.

The barracuda has a long, almost cylindrical, and muscular body, massive jaws, and prominent canine teeth with

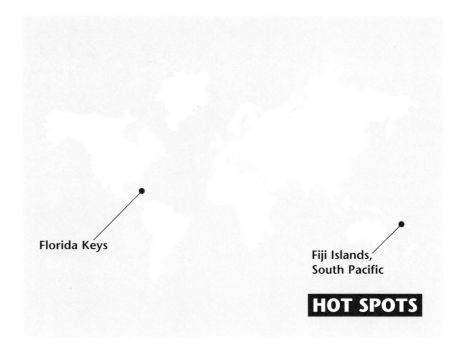

Florida Keys

Fiji Islands, South Pacific

HOT SPOTS

wickedly sharp points and edges. The relatively small first and second dorsal fins are widely separated, and the first dorsal fin is often folded away, out of sight, when the fish is cruising. The barracuda's tail is large and moderately forked.

Varying from bright silver to metallic gray on the flanks, with a darker green, blue, or almost black back, the adult great barracuda usually has a series of irregular black or dark gray blotches on its lower flanks, especially back toward the tail. These black spots and blotches help distinguish the great barracuda from the 20 or more smaller species of barracuda found throughout the world.

Habitat and Behavior

Various barracuda species, including the largest of the clan, the great barracuda, are found in all the tropical oceans and seas of the world, except the eastern Pacific. They will also wander into subtropical and even temperate waters at times, particularly when strong currents are running.

Barracudas are found in both offshore and inshore waters, especially around reefs, piers, wrecks, sandy and grassy flats, and wherever shoals of smaller fish congregate. Juvenile and mid-sized barracudas often form schools, but the very largest specimens are almost always loners with a strongly defined territory.

The great barracuda leads a list of over 300 tropical marine fishes suspected of causing ciguatera (a nerve poisoning) when eaten. This toxin is probably accumulated when peak predators such as barracudas eat smaller forage fish that have previously fed upon a poisonous microscopic plant found on some coral reefs. Since there is no simple or safe way to determine whether a particular barracuda carries this toxin, it is best to practice catch-and-release at all times when dealing with this species.

Finding the Heavyweights

The great barracuda is the giant of the family, growing to at least six or seven feet in length and occasionally weighing as much as 90 pounds. The largest barracu-

IGFA RECORD

GREAT BARRACUDA
Weight: 38.55 kg (85 lbs.)
Place: Christmas Island, Republic of Kiribati
Date: April 11, 1992
Angler: John W. Helfrich

It's easy to see why the barracuda is known as the saltwater wolf.

A gaff is a helpful tool for releasing these toothy gamefish.

HOT SPOT

Fiji

The South Pacific paradise of Fiji offers more than just an idyllic holiday. It also boasts some superb saltwater fishing, with a whole host of species, including some of the world's largest barracudas.

Actually not one island but a whole string of them, Fiji offers a balmy climate, fascinating local culture, and safe, well-organized touring. The very best fishing takes place around some of the more remote outlying islands, but there is often fine fishing within a few miles of major resort hotels in centers such as Suva, Nadi, and Pacific Harbor.

In Fiji, barracudas are known as *onga* by the locals, who treat them with considerable caution and respect – not surprising when one considers that Fiji 'cudas commonly reach six feet and 60 pounds!

Barracudas can be taken in the seas around Fiji year-round, and the biggest specimens are usually encountered while trolling or casting large lures near the outer edges of fringing coral reefs. For information on accommodations and fishing guides in Fiji, contact

Sportfishing Travel Network
937 Centre Road, Dept. 2020
Waterdown, Ontario L0R 2H0

das usually are caught offshore by fishermen trolling baits for other species in warm-water areas of the Atlantic. Big fish will frequent the shallows at times, but big water usually means big fish.

Fishing Techniques

Successful fishing methods for barracudas include trolling with plugs, spoons, and live or rigged dead baits. These fish are also taken at anchor or while drifting with live and dead baits of small fish, as well as while casting and retrieving lures, plugs, spoons, and flies. They are not afraid to strike at large baits, and are particularly keen to pursue long, thin, brightly colored baits, lures, and flies that are trolled or retrieved rapidly.

Naturally, a wire leader should always be used when targeting barracuda, although a surprising number of 'cudas are successfully landed without wire, especially when using larger lures or long baits rigged on big hooks.

When you're sight-fishing to 'cudas in shallow or clear water, the cast should not land too near the cruising fish, and should be retrieved well ahead of it at a fast, erratic pace. Barracuda have fine eyesight and are capable of detecting baits and lures from some distance.

A classic catch from the reefs of Turks and Caicos.

A monster 'cuda awaits its next victim.

HOT SPOT

Florida Keys

The Florida Keys offer some of the finest and most readily accessible barracuda fishing in the world. Around the Keys, small to medium 'cudas in the five- to 25-pound range are most likely to be encountered over the flats, along the edges of deeper channels, around grass beds, and close to isolated structural elements such as navigation markers and reef outcrops. Larger 'cudas up to 50 pounds or more tend to stay farther offshore, but some very big barracudas will show up on the flats at times, particularly when other fish are being hooked and fought and create tempting splashes and vibrations to attract the big "sea wolf."

Sight-casting to cruising barracuda in clear, shallow water around the Keys is always exciting, especially when using light spinning or fly tackle. Most reputable Keys guides and skippers have a list of locations where such action is almost always on tap, particularly from October through May each year.

Lodges and fishing guides are almost everywhere in the Keys. For detailed information, contact

Florida Department of Commerce
Room 505, Collins Building
107 W. Gaines
Tallahassee, Florida
32399-2000

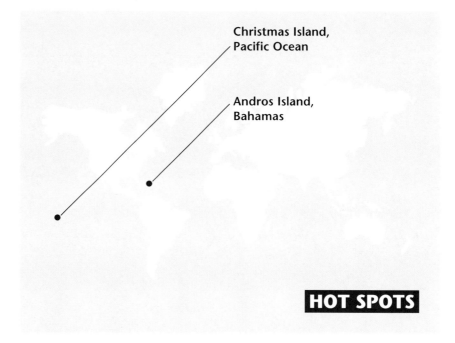

Bonefish

Scientific name: *Albula vulpes*

The bonefish is one of the most highly prized and sought after saltwater gamefish. Widely respected as a brilliant fighter capable of repeated, lightning-fast runs, the bonefish attracts thousands of anglers to the tropics and subtropics each year. Variously known as "his highness and shyness" and the "gray ghost of the flats," the bonefish attracts a reverence and dedication among its followers similar to the respect accorded traditional freshwater species such as Atlantic salmon and brown trout.

As one might expect from their name, bonefish have an abundance of bones, some of which are quite tiny. For this reason, the species is less than popular as table fare. Other bones and vertebrae in the fish's skeleton are massive, as are the muscles attached to them; hence, the fish's blinding speed and acceleration.

The sides and belly of the fish are typically bright, metallic silver, sometimes with a faint overlay of grayish or pale green bars or blotches. The bonefish's back may be gray, light green, or dark green to greeny blue, depending on the color of the seabed over which the fish is feeding. Parts of the fins and the snout may also show a yellowish or dusky color, while a black tip on the snout is quite evident on occasions, as is a dark trailing edge to the tail.

The fish's reflective, counter-shaded coloration makes it almost invisible, even in very clear water. Often, a bonefish's shadow on the sand, or the tip of its tail breaking the surface, is the only indication of its presence.

Christmas Island, Pacific Ocean

Andros Island, Bahamas

HOT SPOTS

Habitat and Behavior

Several different species of bonefish are found in separate regions of the world, mostly in the tropical and subtropical belt on either side of the equator. The most famous is *Albula vulpes* (liter-

IGFA RECORD

BONEFISH
Weight: 8.61 kg (19 lbs.)
Place: Zululand, South Africa
Date: May 26, 1962
Angler: Brian W. Batchelor

This huge 12-pounder will be remembered forever!

ally the "white fox") of the western Atlantic, which occurs in greatest numbers around Florida, through the Caribbean, and southward into Central America, Venezuela, and several other South American countries.

Slightly different fish are found around Pacific islands such as the Hawaiian group and Christmas, Canton, and Ellis islands, as well as on the northeast coast of Australia.

Still another subspecies occurs throughout the Indian Ocean and in isolated pockets along the equatorial and subequatorial coasts of Africa.

The bonefish has a rather strange life cycle, quite unlike that of many other common gamefish, although very similar to the distantly related tarpon and ladyfish. Hatching from tiny eggs, juvenile bonefish begin their lives looking more like baby

eels than fish. Later, they experience a larval stage, growing to a length of about 2½ inches before undergoing a period of metamorphosis, when the eel-like larva shrinks to half its former size, grows tiny fins, and develops into a perfect miniature bonefish. From this point, the bonefish continues to grow and develop quickly, until reaching adulthood and a maximum size of two to 10 pounds. Some bonefish may occasionally reach 13 pounds or more.

Finding the Heavyweights

The most consistent destinations for really large bonefish are Bimini in the Bahamas and Islamorada in Florida. Both locations regularly produce fish more than 13 pounds and account for many of the line- and tippet-class world records.

Bonefish are schooling fish. The smaller ones can often be found in relatively large schools on the flats, particularly in highly productive locations like Venezuela's Los

HOT SPOT

Christmas Island

Part of the extensive but lightly populated island nation of Kiribati, Christmas Island lies in the central Pacific Ocean about 1,000 miles south of Hawaii and just over 100 miles north of the equator. It is the largest coral atoll in the world; a flat, sun-baked plate of limestone surrounded by warm, blue sea, dotted with swaying palm trees and populated by some of the friendliest people in the Pacific Basin. It also happens to be the acknowledged bonefish capital of the world.

Most bonefish at Christmas Island are not especially large, generally running from two to six pounds, but they make up for their small size in sheer numbers. Here, even a relatively inexperienced angler can expect to see 50 to 100 bones a day, cast to perhaps half of them, and hook as many as a dozen. Really experienced bonefish specialists have been known to catch and release 50 fish or more in a single day.

Captain Cook Hotel
This is the only hotel on Christmas Island. Anglers can contract for services and equipment at the hotel itself.

ACCOMMODATIONS
• 24 rooms with private baths
• 12 thatched-roof cottages

MEALS
• Breakfast
• Lunch
• Dinner

EQUIPMENT AVAILABLE
• Flat-bottomed punts transport anglers to certain fishing locations
• Most fishing by wading

RECOMMENDED EQUIPMENT
• Light to medium spinning outfit for casting bait
• Seven- to nine-weight fly outfit with floating or sink-tip line and plenty of backing (minimum 150 yards)
• Selection of nymphs and streamers

SEASON
• Outstanding year-round
• Best fishing: March to September

CONTACT
Fishing International Inc.
4010 Montecito Avenue
Santa Rosa, California 95405

One of the most classic scenes in bonefishing, an angler stalking the shallows under a guide's direction.

Perfectly camouflaged, bonefish search the shallows for small crabs.

Roques or the Christmas Island flats. Larger bonefish tend to form smaller schools – groups or pods of two to six individuals – although single fish are not uncommon in many localities.

Bonefish are often seen rooting in the sand for mollusks and crustaceans, with their tail tips breaking the surface of the shallow water in an action commonly known as tailing. At other times, groups or schools of bonefish will plow through an area of the bottom, stirring up silt and marl to form a muddy cloud or smudge in the water, an action known as mudding. When mudding, bonefish can be relatively easy to approach and catch.

Often, the very largest bonefish hunt in slightly deeper water along the outer edges of the flats, or in channels running between shallow areas. These big fish may enter shallow flats water for only an hour or two each day, often on a rising tide at dawn or dusk.

Fishing Techniques

Most fishing for bonefish is done with spinning rods and fly rods, either from a skiff or while wading across tidal flats. Polarized sunglasses, a long-

HOT SPOT

Andros Island, Bahamas

- Lunch
- Dinner

EQUIPMENT AVAILABLE
- Guides provide flats boats with outboards

RECOMMENDED EQUIPMENT
- Light to medium spinning outfit for casting bait
- Seven- to nine-weight fly outfit with floating or sink-tip line and plenty of backing (minimum 150 yards)
- Selection of nymphs and streamers

SEASON
- Year-round
- Best fishing: April, May, June

CONTACT
Angler Adventures
P.O. Box 872
Old Lyme, Connecticut 06371

Bahamas Tourism
121 Bloor Street East
Suite 1101
Toronto, Ontario M4W 3M5

Andros Island is acknowledged as an angler's paradise, especially for those keen on pursuing bonefish. The Bahamas may not have the same vast schools of bonefish as Christmas Island, but they certainly have some very big bones.

Cargill Creek Fishing Lodge
Cargill Creek Fishing Lodge offers world-class fishing on famed Andros Island of the Bahamas. The lodge atmosphere is relaxed and informal, with full facilities for discriminating anglers.

ACCOMMODATIONS
- 4 single, 7 doubles, 3 cottages (all air conditioned)

MEALS
- Breakfast

---

billed cap, and sharp eyes are necessary, though these fish can sometimes be caught blind, especially when using natural baits or small jigs.

Best natural offerings are live or very fresh shrimp, sand bugs and crabs, pieces of clam meat, conch, or squid, often fished in conjunction with a sparse chum trail. These baits should be presented on light line with little or no additional casting weight.

The most productive lure patterns are small, lead-head jigs with natural fur or feather tails or small, soft-plastic grubs. Small crankbaits and even spoons will also produce.

When it comes to flies, the best patterns are shrimp or crab imitations tied on No. 6 to No. 2 hooks. Some productive designs include the Crazy Charlie, Nasty Charlie, Chico's Special, small Bendbacks, and Clouser's Deep Minnow.

Bonefish are free of teeth, spines, and spikes, and are one of the easiest of all saltwater gamefish to handle. This fact combined with their poor eating qualities means that almost all bonefishing is a catch-and-release sport, helping to ensure the future of this wonderful marine species.

Torpedo shaped, unbelievably fast, unbelievably powerful!

Dolphin

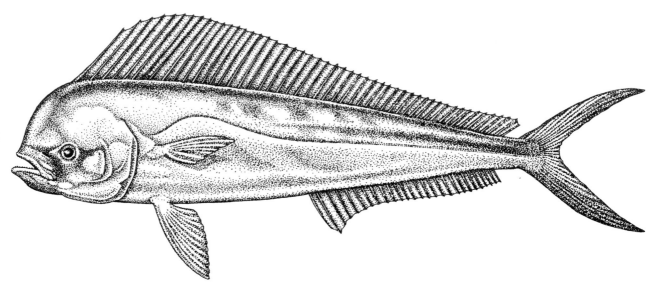

Scientific name: *Coryphaena hippurus*

The dolphin, also known as the mahi-mahi and dorado, is one of the ocean's most beautiful and spectacular offshore species. A true bony fish, it is unrelated to the highly intelligent marine mammals known as dolphins or porpoises. Dolphin anglers are not out to hook Flipper.

Dolphin are a medium-sized gamefish revered by offshore anglers all over the world for their glorious appearance, superb eating qualities, and exciting runs and jumps when hooked. They are almost always a welcome catch, even when they strike baits or lures intended for larger species such as marlin, sailfish, and tuna.

Dolphin are distinctive in both shape and coloration. One of the most beautiful fish in the sea, they have colors that are quite variable and defy a simple description. Generally, when swimming through the water, the dolphin exhibits a rich, iridescent blue or blue-green back

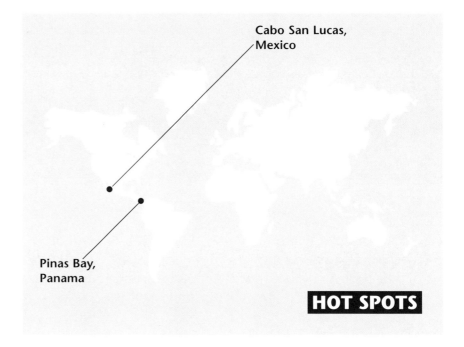

Cabo San Lucas, Mexico

Pinas Bay, Panama

HOT SPOTS

and upper flanks, with gold, blue-gold or silvery lower flanks, and a silvery white or yellow belly. The fish's sides are sprinkled with a mixture of dark and light spots, which range from black to electric blue to gold. The dorsal fin is a very rich blue, and the anal fin may be either gold or silver, while the other fins are generally yellowish, edged with blue.

When the dolphin is removed from the water, its

colors commonly change and fluctuate quite rapidly between blue, green, and yellow. After death, the fish usually turns uniformly yellow or silvery gray, with a sprinkling of darker spots on the flanks.

Habitat and Behavior

Found worldwide in all tropical, subtropical, and warm temperate seas, the dolphin is highly pelagic and migrato-

In large male dolphins, the front of the head becomes very high, almost vertical.

ry, preferring to swim near the surface in clean, warm, blue water. Although very occasionally caught from long ocean piers, or in green, shallower areas closer to shore, dolphin are basically an offshore species found over deep, oceanic waters, particularly in areas with strong currents.

Dolphin are extremely fast swimmers and prey primarily on flying fish and squid, as well as on other small species such as anchovies, balao (ballyhoo), runners, and mackerel. They feed actively and frequently, growing rapidly during their short four- to six-year life. Since dolphin are themselves a favorite meal for marlin,

big tuna, and some of the faster ocean-going sharks, natural mortality rates are very high.

Finding the Heavyweights

Large male dolphin, called bulls, have high, almost vertical foreheads, while the female, or cow, dolphin's forehead is much lower and more rounded. Bulls grow considerably larger than cows, occasionally reaching six feet and 90 pounds.

Smaller dolphin usually roam in schools, with smaller fish in the two- to 20-pound range the most abundant. On the other hand, very large bull dolphin are

IGFA RECORD

DOLPHIN
Weight: 39.46 kg (87 lbs.)
Place: Papagallo Gulf, Costa Rica
Date: Sept. 25, 1976
Angler: Manuel Salazar

Dolphins cruise the warm water of the Gulf Stream in search of smaller fish and squid.

These acrobatic fish are aggressive and will strike a variety of artificial lures.

HOT SPOT

Pinas Bay, Panama

Pinas Bay, in the Central American nation of Panama, is famous for record-sized dolphin, particularly for anglers targeting the species on light spinning tackle or fly rods.

December is by far the best month for catching heavy-weight dolphin at Pinas Bay, although November and January also produce fine fishing. For details on guides and accommodations, contact

Sportfishing Travel Network 937 Centre Road, Dept. 2020 Waterdown, Ontario L0R 2H0

sometimes encountered singly or in the company of just three or four adult females.

Fishing Techniques

Dolphin have a particularly strong affinity for floating or suspended objects in the water, such as navigation buoys, clumps of drifting seaweed, and logs. Skillful anglers know that distinct current edges and weed-lines are hot areas for dolphin.

Productive dolphin techniques include trolling with small- to medium-sized lures and plugs, live baits, or rigged dead baits (particularly balao and mullet). Drifting with similar baits is also productive. Casting at and around objects floating in the current with lures, flies, or baits can be a very exciting and effective way of targeting dolphin, and if the first one hooked is kept in the water, it will often attract the entire school, drawing them near enough to be caught by casting with spin or fly tackle.

Once hooked, dolphin frequently leap high from the water or tail-walk across the waves, darting first in one direction, then in another.

It is believed that free-swimming dolphin can reach speeds of up to 50 miles per hour over short bursts, and most anglers who have seen the way these speedsters can strip line from a fishing reel would have little trouble believing it.

When the fish is caught, the color fluctuates rapidly. It may be blue, green, or yellow.

HOT SPOT

Cabo San Lucas, Mexico

Cabo San Lucas, on the southern tip of Baja California, Mexico, is a favorite destination for anglers from all over the world. Renowned for its superb marlin and tuna fishing, Cabo also produces world-class dolphin, particularly from June through October, when the waters are the warmest.

Many dolphin are hooked while trolling baits and lures for marlin, although anglers also enjoy fine action by working the current edges and weed lines with light tackle. Normally anglers troll until one fish is hooked, then quickly cast lures or flies while the first dolphin is brought toward the boat.

For information on dolphin fishing in Mexico, contact

Mexican Department
of Fisheries
2550 Fifth Avenue,
Suite 1001
San Diego, California
92103-6622

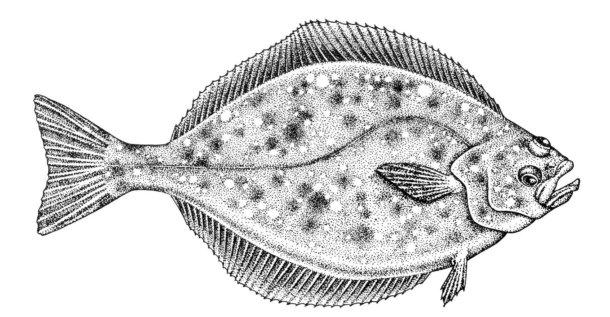

Scientific names: *Hippoglossus hippoglossus* (Atlantic Halibut) and *H. stenolepis* (Pacific Halibut)

Halibut

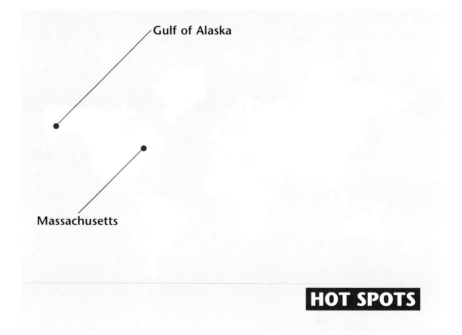

Gulf of Alaska

Massachusetts

HOT SPOTS

Several species of the very large flatfish called halibut are found in the cool waters of the northern hemisphere. The biggest and best known are the Atlantic halibut and the Pacific halibut. The somewhat smaller California halibut (*Paralichthys californicus*) is found along sections of the west coast of the United States, particularly off the northern and central parts of the state of California.

Halibut are highly prized as table fish and support an active commercial fishery. They are also popular with anglers, when they enter relatively shallow waters close to shore.

Like most flatfish, small halibut swim upright in the water and have an eye on either side of their heads. As they grow, halibut begin to swim on one side, and one of their eyes slowly migrates around the head to join the other on what ultimately becomes the fish's upper surface.

The halibut's teeth are strong and equally well developed on both sides of the jaws. Coloration is uniformly dark brown or gray on the fish's upper surface, often with small, lighter colored spots and blotches. They are typically white and relatively featureless on the underside, although some specimens, often called cherrybellies, have a distinct reddish tint on their lower surface.

Habitat and Behavior

The Atlantic halibut (*H. hippoglossus*) inhabits cold ocean waters throughout the North Atlantic, as well as the seas around Iceland and Greenland. It is also found in very deep, cold waters as far south as Virginia on the American side of the Atlantic and east to southwest Ireland on the European side. This species does not occur in near-freezing polar waters, as many people believe, but is replaced there by the Greenland halibut (*Reinhardtius hippoglossoides*).

Pacific halibut are found in the cold waters of the North Pacific from the Bering Sea south to about Santa Rosa Island in California, and as far south as northern Japan and the Okhotsk Sea on the Asian side of the Pacific.

Halibut of both species are highly migratory. Tagging programs have shown that some adult halibut travel 2,000 miles or more during their lives, although other individuals appear to remain quite near to their spawning grounds.

In cooler, northern areas, large halibut can be found in relatively shallow waters, but in the warmer southern portions of their range they

IGFA RECORD

HALIBUT, PACIFIC
Weight: 166.92 kg (368 lbs.)
Place: Gustavus Alaska, U.S.A.
Date: July 5, 1991
Angler: Celia H. Ducitt

often swim in water as deep as about 3,000 feet.

Halibut are predatory and mainly hunt other fish such as haddock, cod, herring, mackerel, red fish, and capelin, as well as crabs, squid, and mollusks. Usually, they swim very near the sea bed, but will occasionally rise into mid-water to pursue their prey.

Finding the Heavyweights

The Atlantic halibut is one of the biggest fish found in the

IGFA RECORD

HALIBUT, ATLANTIC
Weight: 115.78 kg (255 lbs. 4 oz.)
Place: Gloucester, Mass., U.S.A.
Date: July 28, 1989
Angler: Sonny Manley

One of the halibut's unique characteristics: both eyes are on the same side of the body.

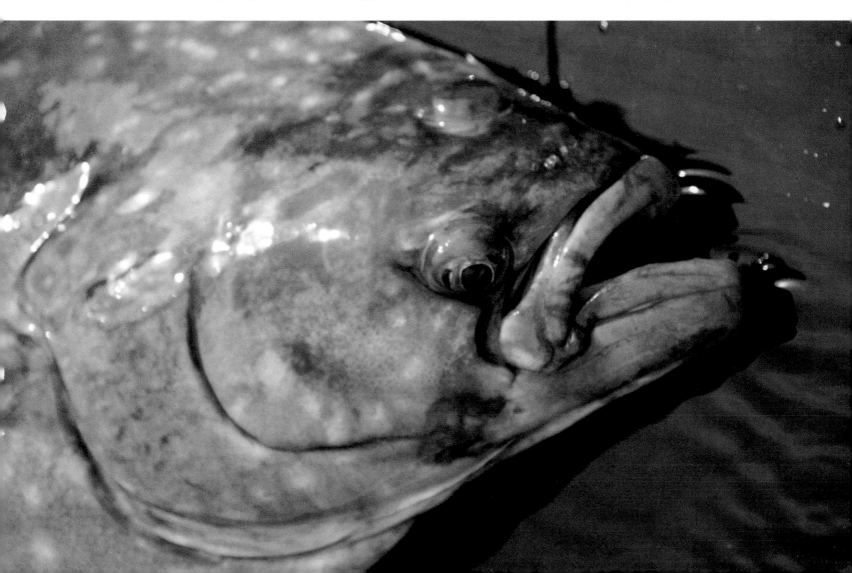

sea. The largest recorded specimen was taken off Sweden by commercial fishermen and weighed a whopping 720 pounds. By 1995 the heaviest rod-and-reel capture officially recorded by the IGFA was a 255-pound fish taken off Gloucester, Massachusetts, in 1989 – quite a difference. No doubt many much larger fish have been hooked and lost, which speaks volumes about just how tough these fish are to handle.

The Pacific halibut resembles its Atlantic cousin and also grows to impressive sizes. Females of the Pacific species reach top weights of at least 470 pounds, and may live to 45 years. In contrast, the less-abundant and slower-growing males generally do not exceed 40 pounds, and their maximum life expectancy appears to be about 25 years or less. Alaska and the Queen Charlotte Islands of British Columbia produce quality fish.

Large halibut of both species often exceed six feet in length and may occasionally top the eight-foot mark. Such giants may be as much as four or five feet wide. In a way, hooking a halibut is somewhat like hooking a barn door. Give that door several hundred pounds of muscle, then put it in very deep water – often with heavy current – and you have an idea what you're in for.

A really big halibut is an immensely powerful creature, capable of putting up a sustained battle. Halibut over 70 or 80 pounds are also difficult to handle at the boat and have been known to injure anglers and damage boat fittings with their wild thrashing.

Fishing Techniques

Halibut are most commonly caught while drift-fishing with natural baits and moderately heavy tackle, either on or near the bottom. Since halibut will feed actively in mid-

HOT SPOT

Massachusetts

Anglers chasing heavyweight Atlantic halibut should head for the northern Massachusetts ports of Marblehead, Gloucester Harbor, and Newburyport, all of which lie between Cape Cod and the Maine border.

Reef and wreck boats heading offshore from these ports during summer and early fall in search of cod, hake, pollock, and other saltwater prizes occasionally encounter big Atlantic halibut. Sometimes, these giant flatfish grab baits intended for smaller fare, or even hit hooked fish and become hooked or snared themselves. To target big halibut, fish over known feeding grounds use sturdy tackle and large baits.

While halibut in excess of 40 pounds are possible just about any time, the largest ones are usually caught in July.

For information on accommodations and fishing guides, contact

Massachusetts Tourism Office
100 Cambridge Street,
13th Floor
Boston, Massachusetts 02202

HOT SPOT

Gulf of Alaska

Cove, Gustavus, Sitka, Juneau, Petersbug, Wrangell, and Ketchikan. Anglers fishing offshore from all these Alaskan harbors regularly catch halibut in excess of 100 pounds, with the occasional giant of 200 pounds or more turning up each season.

The best time to go? It's hard to beat the summer and early fall, from mid-June until the end of September. However, anglers boat impressive halibut here as late as early November. For details on fishing guides and accommodations, contact

The Gulf of Alaska and its many inshore islands, bays, and straits have produced some of the largest Pacific halibut ever taken on rod and reel. Especially productive halibut ports within this vast area include Anchorage, Homer, Seward, Valdez, Yakutat, Elfin

Alaska Division of Tourism
P.O. Box 110801
Juneau, Alaska
99811-0801

water, big ones are often caught while jigging with large diamond jigs and pirks, while others are hooked accidentally on cut-plug herring and similar baits trolled or mooched for salmon.

Frequently, salmon tackle proves too light to handle very large halibut, and many of these fish smash the angler's gear and escape. Occasionally, a lucky and skillful salmon angler will

manage to boat a giant halibut after a long and memorable battle on relatively light line. These incidental captures account for many of the line-class records currently on the charts.

Mackerel

Scientific name: *Scomberomorus cavalla* (King Mackerel)
and *S. maculatus* (Spanish Mackerel)

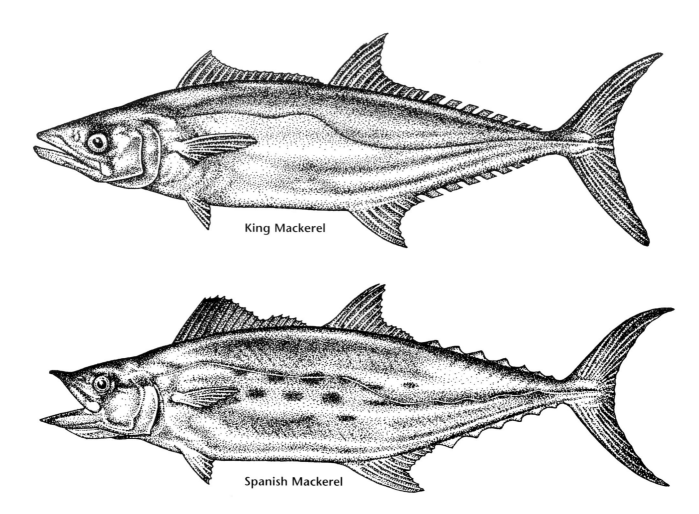

King Mackerel

Spanish Mackerel

Many species of mackerel from the family Scombridae are found in the tropical, sub-tropical, and warm temperate seas of the world, but the two of importance to anglers are the king mackerel of the western Atlantic and the narrow-barred Spanish mackerel (or Pacific Spanish mackerel) of the Indian and Pacific oceans.

All of the Scombridae mackerels are sleek, fast-swimming predators with powerful jaws and very sharp teeth. They bear a superficial resemblance to the unrelated wahoo, but may be distinguished by their tail shape and lateral line configuration. Wahoo have much shorter and more upright tail lobes

and a lateral line that dips distinctively below the middle of the first dorsal fin, much farther forward than it does on either of the big mackerel species.

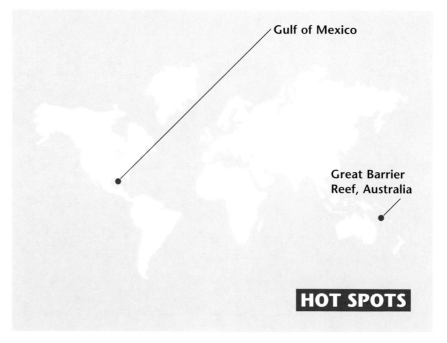

Gulf of Mexico

Great Barrier Reef, Australia

HOT SPOTS

Habitat and Behavior: King Mackerel

Found only in tropical, sub-tropical, and warm temperate waters of the western Atlantic

Catching mackerel on light tackle in offshore waters is a lot of fun.

IGFA RECORD

MACKEREL, KING
Weight: 40.82 (90 lbs.)
Place: Key West, Florida, U.S.A.
Date: Feb. 16, 1976
Angler: Norton I. Thomton

larger specimens are mostly found farther offshore, around wrecks, buoys, coral reefs, weed lines, and other structures where prey, such as smaller fish and squid, is most abundant.

Schools vary considerably in size. Smaller mackerel often form large groups, while the biggest fish are usually loners.

Habitat and Behavior: Pacific Spanish Mackerel

The Pacific Spanish mackerel is similar in appearance to the Atlantic king mackerel, and fills a similar ecological niche in its part of the world. However, the Spanish mackerel is found only in the warmer waters of the western Pacific and Indian oceans, from the Fiji Islands west around the northern

Ocean, king mackerel occasionally range as far north as Maine, but they are far more common farther south, off Virginia, the Carolinas, Georgia, and Florida. They also occur extensively in the Gulf of Mexico and along the east coast of South America as far as Rio de Janeiro. King mackerel are most abundant around southern Florida during the winter months, when northern waters drop below about 70°F.

This migratory species is constantly on the move, and stocks wintering in Florida may migrate west to Texas and as far north as Virginia or Maryland during summer. Some king mackerel are also found around southern Florida in the spring and early summer months.

A coastal, schooling species, king mackerel usually swim in water from 10 to 20 fathoms (60 to 180 feet). Occasionally they are caught from ocean piers and the shoreline around inlets, but

HOT SPOT

Great Barrier Reef, Australia

Australia's Great Barrier Reef, which stretches for thousands of miles along the northeastern coastline of the continent, is one of the natural wonders of the world. It also hosts some of the world's finest saltwater fishing.

Big Spanish mackerel are just one of many species actively pursued by offshore anglers in that part of the southwestern Pacific known as the Coral Sea. From Moreton Bay and Brisbane in the south to Cairns, Cooktown, and Lizard Island in the far north, potential record-breaking Spanish mackerel are available in all months of the year.

Generally speaking, the mackerel run is at its best in the north of this region during the southern winter (June, July, and August), with the action moving steadily southward throughout spring, and peaking off Brisbane and the Gold Coast in the Australian summer (December, January, and February). Good mackerel are taken off northern ports such as Cairns and Townsville right through the year.

Many fine charter boats operate along the coast of the northeastern Australian state of Queensland, offering visiting anglers from all over the world a chance to work these fish-rich waters for big mackerel. Charter fleets are available in both areas for visiting anglers. For information on guides, charter boats, and so on, contact

Angling Adventures
P.O. Box 4094
Geelong, VIC, 3200 Australia

half of Australia and across the Indian Ocean to the Red Sea and east Africa. Spanish mackerel occasionally migrate through the Suez Canal into the eastern part of the Mediterranean.

Spanish mackerel are popular with local fishermen wherever they are found, and have a string of regional names. In Fiji, they are called walu, while Australians refer to them as narrow-barred Spanish mackerel, or Spaniards, for short. Pacific Spanish mackerel have similar habits and life cycles to their Atlantic cousins, but will sometimes stray into slightly deeper water than will king mackerel.

Finding the Heavyweights

Although many tropical mackerel are relatively small fish, rarely exceeding three feet and 12 pounds, both the king and Spanish mackerel grow much larger, occasionally topping six feet in length and more than 90 pounds. Pacific Spanish mackerel over 100 pounds have been taken by commercial fishermen. Even larger ones have been reported from Korea.

Fishing Techniques

Fishing methods for big mackerel include trolling, anchoring, or drifting. Mackerel anglers fish either deep or on the surface, using strip baits, lures, or small whole baits. Balao, mullet, jacks, herring, pinfish, croakers, shrimp, spoons, feathers, jigs, and plugs have all proven effective on big mackerel under various conditions, as have combinations such as feather jigs or skirted

The mackerel grows rapidly and schools according to size.

heads rigged over a strip bait or a whole balao. Chumming also works well at times to attract and hold these fish in a specific area.

Big mackerel make fast, slashing attacks on baits and lures. Very sharp hooks and tail-rigged stinger hooks are often necessary. Once on the line, large mackerel make extremely fast, long, and determined runs, but generally tire after one or two such dashes. Even on relatively light tackle, battles with big mackerel are usually much shorter than those of tuna, trevally, or amberjack.

The king and Spanish mackerel are very important from both a commercial and sporting perspective. Their flesh is firm and of excellent quality. However, Spanish mackerel have been linked with occurrences of ciguatera poisoning in Australian and South Pacific waters, and for this reason, larger specimens are not eaten in those areas where the ciguatera toxin is common.

HOT SPOT
Gulf of Mexico

The Gulf of Mexico produces some of North America's finest and most consistent king mackerel fishing, particularly during the late fall and winter, when fish migrate into these warm, shallow waters to escape the cooler currents farther east and north.

Ports along the west coast of Florida, Alabama, Mississippi, west of the delta in Louisiana, and right through Texas to Corpus Christi and the Padre Island National Seashore all produce superb king mackerel action at times, with many local skippers and guides targeting these highly prized fish for several months each season.

Some of the best king mackerel fishing in the gulf occurs well offshore, around oil drilling platforms, rigs, navigation markers, and patches of reef. At such hot spots, encounters with kings in the 40- to 60-pound range are a strong possibility, with exceptional specimens to 80 pounds and more occasionally turning up.

For information on fishing the Gulf of Mexico, contact

Sportfishing Travel Network
937 Centre Road
Waterdown, Ontario L0R 2H0

Because of their sharp teeth, always use wire leaders.

Marlin

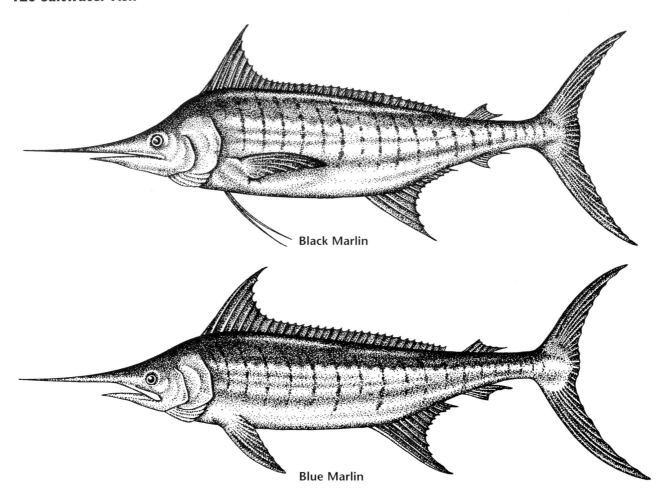

Black Marlin

Blue Marlin

Scientific names: *Makaira indica* (Black Marlin), *M. nigricans* (Blue Marlin), *Tetrapturus audax* (Striped Marlin), *T. albidus* (White Marlin)

Marlin are among the largest of all true fish. Only the sharks grow larger than the biggest Marlin. Four distinct species of marlin are found in the warm oceans of the world: the black, the blue, the striped, and the white. For record-book purposes, blue marlin are divided into two subspecies: the Atlantic blue marlin and Indo-Pacific blue marlin. Geography notwithstanding, these two subspecies are virtually identical in terms of physiology, life cycle, and general behavior. To most anglers, they're one and the same.

The black marlin is the only marlin with rigid, wing-like pectoral fins that cannot be folded flat against the

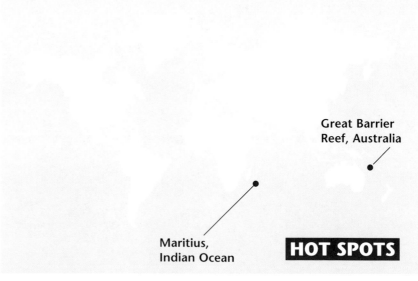

Great Barrier Reef, Australia

Maritius, Indian Ocean

HOT SPOTS

body. Only very small black marlin, under about 60 pounds, may have semi-flexible fins. The black marlin has very short ventral fins, which almost never exceed 12 inches in length. The first dorsal fin is also the lowest of any billfish, usually less than 50 percent of the body depth.

Despite the name, black marlin exhibit a range of colorations. The fish's upper back is usually black, gunmetal blue, or slate gray, changing abruptly to silvery white below the lateral line. When feeding or leaping, black marlin may display light blue vertical stripes on their sides, and spots or patches of lavender blue on the fins, but these fade rapidly after death.

The pectoral fins of blue marlin are never rigid, even after death, and can be folded completely flat against the sides. The dorsal fin is high and pointed, rather than rounded, as is the blue's relatively large anal fin.

The blue marlin's back is usually dark cobalt blue, while the flanks and belly show silvery white. Light blue or lavender vertical stripes are often evident on the fish's sides, but these may fade quickly after death, and are never as distinct as those of the smaller striped marlin.

The most obvious characteristic of the striped marlin is its very high, pointed first dorsal fin, which normally equals or exceeds the fish's greatest body depth. Even in the largest specimens this fin measures at least 90 percent of the body depth. Like the dorsal fin, the anal and pectoral fins are pointed. The pectorals are flat and movable, and can easily be folded against the sides, even after death. The striped marlin's bill is also longer and thinner than that of other marlin.

The striped marlin is steely blue on the back, fading to bluish silver on the upper flanks and white below the lateral line. There are usually a number of iridescent blue spots on the fins

and 12 to 14 pale blue or lavender vertical stripes on the sides. These stripes are more prominent than those of any other marlin, and do not fade after death.

The most characteristic features of the white marlin are the rounded tips of the fish's pectoral fins, first dorsal fin, and first anal fin. The first dorsal fin resembles that of the striped marlin, in that it is usually as high or higher than the greatest body depth. However, it is much more rounded at the top than that of the striped marlin. In overall appearance, the white marlin is generally lighter in color than any other marlin, and tends to show more green on the back and flanks than the other species. Light blue or lavender vertical bars may also appear on the fish's flanks, particularly when it is hooked or feeding, and some fish may have a scattering of black or purple spots on the first dorsal and anal fins. Generally, these markings fade after death.

Habitat and Behavior: The Black Marlin

With its short, baseball-bat bill, deep, thick body, and "don't mess with me" disposition, the mighty black marlin has been dubbed the rhinoceros of the sea. An aggressive, hard-fighting gamefish, the black marlin is found in the tropical, subtropical, and warm temperate areas of the Indian and Pacific oceans. In more tropical areas, the black marlin's distribution is relatively continuous throughout

IGFA RECORD

MARLIN, BLACK
Weight: 707.61 kg (1,560 lbs.)
Place: Cabo Blanco, Peru
Date: Aug. 4, 1953
Angler: Alfred C. Glassell Jr.

Marlin are highly valued by sport fishermen because of their size and spectacular fight.

open, offshore waters. It is most abundant in coastal areas, particularly near islands and reef edges. In temperate waters, black marlin occur more sporadically and appear to be closely tied to the annual ebb and flow of warm currents flowing north and south from the equator. Their diet consists largely of squid and smaller pelagic fish such as tuna, mackerel, dol-

HOT SPOT

Great Barrier Reef, Australia

A stretch of the outer Great Barrier Reef off northeastern Australia is renowned as the giant black marlin hot spot of the world. Each year, from late September until early December, thousands of big black marlin gather from Townsville or Cairns, north to Lizard Island as part of their annual spawning ritual. Boats operating from these ports, or from large, comfortable mother ships that cruise the outer reef edges, regularly tangle with black marlin in the 100- to 800-pound range.

Marlin fishing in this area is almost always done with 80- and 130-pound-test lines, trolling carefully rigged dead baits of scad, mackerel, or tuna. However, in recent years some fine catches have also been made using large lures.

The best bet for anglers bent on taking on a giant Australian black marlin is to use the services of an established booking agent. Contact

Angling Adventures
P.O. Box 4094
Geelong, VIC, 3200 Australia

This organization specializes in arranging big-game adventures and can handle all arrangements for a first-class trip.

phin, and flying fish. Black marlin have been known to swallow prey weighing up to 10 percent of their own body weight.

Habitat and Behavior: The Blue Marlin

Blue marlin are found in tropical and warm temperate oceanic waters of the Atlantic, Pacific, and Indian oceans, being more prolific in the western portions of each of these seas than in the eastern parts. Off North America, blue marlin occur throughout the deeper offshore waters of the Gulf of Mexico and northward along the eastern seaboard at least as far as Maine. They are more common off Florida, Georgia, the Carolinas, and Virginia, as well as around Cuba and throughout the Caribbean. Superb blue marlin fishing also takes place in the mid-Atlantic, around the Azores and the Canary Islands. In the Pacific, the Hawaiian Islands is an acknowledged hot spot for big blue marlin, while farther west, Mauritius has some of the finest blue marlin fishing in the Indian Ocean. The blue marlin is known to feed on squid and pelagic fish, including tuna and mackerel. A powerful, aggressive fighter, the blue marlin can run hard and long, sound deep, and leap high into the air in a seemingly inexhaustible display of strength and stamina. It is regarded by many experts as the hardest-fighting of all billfish.

Habitat and Behavior: The Striped Marlin

Striped marlin are pelagic migratory fish found in tropical, subtropical, and warm temperate waters of the Indian and Pacific oceans. They appear to move toward the equator during the colder months and away again during the warmest parts of the year. At the maximum extent of this annual migration, striped marlin are found in waters cooler than that frequented by any other marlin. Like other marlin, the striped marlin is highly predatory, feeding extensively on pilchards, anchovies, mackerel, sauries, flying fish, squid, and whatever else it can catch. Striped marlin can often be caught quite close to shore. Although they lack the size and weight of the blue or the black marlin, they tend to be more acrobatic, often spending more time in the air than in the water once hooked. In addition to long runs and tailwalks, the striped marlin will frequently "greyhound" across the surface, making up to a dozen or more long, graceful leaps one after another.

Habitat and Behavior: The White Marlin

The lightly built and highly agile white marlin is found throughout the Atlantic Ocean, from about latitude 35° south to 45° north. This range includes the Gulf of Mexico, the Caribbean Sea, and the western Mediterranean. Stray whites have also been recorded well outside this area. While usually found in deep, offshore areas, white marlin will sometimes come much closer to the coast, where the water may be as shallow as 10 fathoms (60 feet).

Finding the Heavyweights

The two heavyweights of the marlin clan are the black and the blue. Adult females of both species regularly top 800 pounds, and fish in excess of 1,000 pounds – called granders by anglers – are not uncommon. In exceptional cases, black marlin may approach 2,000 pounds, while the Indo-Pacific blue has an even greater growth potential, possibly topping an amazing 2,500 pounds. Stories of boat-sized marlin wrecking equipment after day-long fights, and of precision reels literally burning out – smoke billowing from their drags – are legendary.

To put their mammoth size in perspective, consider that the large striped marlin is just a middleweight in this family, despite the fact that it commonly reaches 220 pounds and sometimes attains twice that weight. At the lightweight end of the scale is the white marlin, a relatively small gamefish (at least compared with its enormous relatives) that seldom tops 100 pounds and has a maximum growth potential of less than 200 pounds.

The female black marlin grows faster and reaches a much larger size than her male counterpart. Black marlin heavier than about 300 pounds are almost always females. Today, the acknowledged giant black marlin capital of the world is a stretch of outer Great Barrier Reef between Cairns and Lizard Island, in northeastern Australia.

Very large striped marlin over 350 pounds are mostly taken from New Zealand or Australian waters. Those caught off Mexico and along the southern Californian coast, although possibly more abundant, are usually much smaller, with most weighing between 100 and 200 pounds.

Fishing Techniques

Fishing methods for marlin include trolling with large whole or cut baits such as mackerel, bonito, flying fish, balao, and squid, or trolling with a range of artificial lures such as Konaheads and pushers. Live bait is also very effective at times.

Anglers use a wide range of tackle when pursuing marlin, from light spinning rods and 12- to 20-pound-test line for fish under 200 pounds, up to 80- and 130-pound-class equipment on the largest fish. A strong, abrasion-resistant leader of heavy nylon or wire keeps the fish from slicing the main line with its hard, sandpaper-like mouth and bill.

While marlin – especially small to mid-sized fish – are perfectly edible and quite delicious, an increasing number of anglers are choosing to tag and live-release their fish. This growing conservation

HOT SPOT

Mauritius

The relatively small but densely populated island of Mauritius lies in the southwest Indian Ocean, east of Madagascar. Its exotic culture blends European traditions with African and Indian influences. While European sportfishermen, especially those from Britain, France, and Germany, have long been aware of the gamefishing potential of Mauritius, it has come to international prominence only during the past decade, most notably as a result of the giant Indo-Pacific blue marlin so frequently encountered in its offshore waters.

Blues to 1,400 pounds and more have been recorded here, along with more abundant smaller fish in the 200- to 500-pound range. Other exciting targets include yellowfin tuna, record-class skipjack, and some huge mako sharks.

Fine fishing opportunities are available year-round from Mauritian ports such as Black River, although blue-marlin action peaks in December. Some of the island's most prestigious fishing tournaments are staged at that time. For information on them, and on Mauritian marlin fishing in general, write

Mauritius Government Tourist Office
New York Penta Hotel
18th Floor
401 Seventh Avenue
New York, New York 10001

ethic is helping to maintain strong stocks of these noble and popular gamefish.

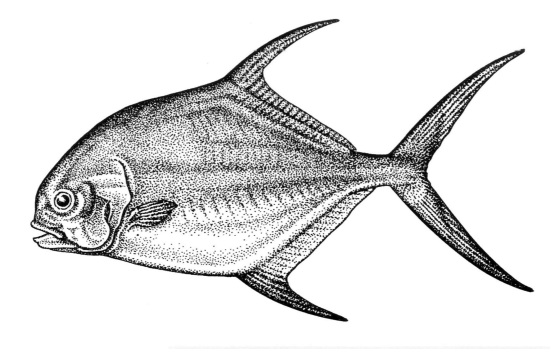

Permit (Atlantic)

Scientific name: *Trachinotus falcatus*

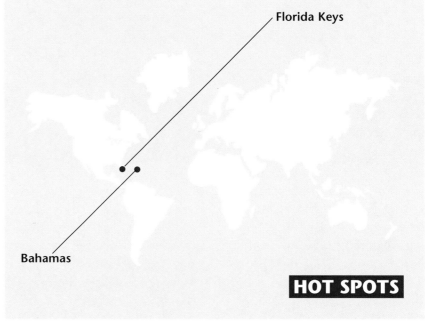

Florida Keys

Bahamas

HOT SPOTS

If the bonefish is the bread-and-butter fish of the flats, then the permit is the glittering jackpot to which all inshore anglers aspire. Permit are even more cautious and sharp-eyed than bonefish and, once hooked, fight just as hard on a pound-for-pound basis, making long, fast, and determined runs. Although bonefish rarely top 10 pounds in most areas, permit regularly reach weights of 20 pounds.

At one time considered impossible to catch on fly gear, permit are the ultimate prize for saltwater fly casters. With the advent of new patterns and techniques, including chumming over fish-rich wrecks and reefs, many more devotees of the long rod have been able to cash in on the permit bonanza. Still, the art of finding, stalking, and catching permit in shallow water, particularly with fly tackle, remains one of modern angling's greatest challenges.

The permit is a bright, silvery or silver-white fish with dusky, orange or yellowish fins. The back is usually blue or gray, while the ventral fins and the front edge of the anal fin may be tinged orange or yellow, and there is often an irregular, triangular patch of yellow ahead of the anal fin.

The permit is similar in appearance to the common or Florida pompano (*T. carolinus*), but may be distinguished from that smaller, more abundant fish in several ways: Permit have fewer soft rays in their dorsal and anal fins (one spine and just 17 to 21 soft rays, compared with 22 to 27 soft rays in the pompano), and the permit's body is somewhat laterally compressed, normally with the fish's second and third ribs quite evident (and often as thick as a man's thumb).

Habitat and Behavior

True Atlantic permit are found only in the western

Atlantic Ocean from Massachusetts south to Brazil. This range includes most of the Gulf of Mexico, the Bahamas, the Caribbean, and the West Indies. A similar but quite distinct species – the Pacific permit – also occurs in parts of the Pacific and Indian oceans, where it has various regional names including snub-nosed dart and oyster-cracker.

Permit are essentially shallow-water fish, favoring sandy flats and broken reefs in water less than 70 feet. They normally travel in schools of 10 or more fish, although they may occasionally be seen in even greater concentrations. Like many other species, really big permit tend to become more solitary with age, and fish over 30 pounds are most often encountered singly or in pairs.

Permit feed in much the same manner as bonefish, rooting and nuzzling in the sand or marl on shallow flats, although they rarely stir up as much mud as bones do. The permit's diet consists primarily of small mollusks, crustaceans (especially crabs), sea urchins, and, less commonly, smaller fish. They are often attracted to areas where the bottom has been disturbed by the activities of other creatures, such as feeding bonefish, snappers, or stingrays.

Finding the Heavyweights

The greatest concentrations of permit are found off southern Florida, particularly in the Keys, and it is here that the very largest specimens are taken. Several permit in excess of 50 pounds have also been recorded from Florida waters, and the maximum growth potential of the fish in this region may be more than 60 pounds.

This potential IGFA record was released after weighing in at 39 pounds.

IGFA RECORD

PERMIT
Weight: 23.35 kg (51 lbs. 8 oz.)
Place: Lake Worth, Florida, U.S.A.
Date: April 28, 1978
Angler: William M. Kenney

Fishing Techniques

Fishing methods for permit include sight-casting to visible fish in shallow water, bottom-fishing with bait, fishing over inshore wrecks and reefs with chum; and jigging, lure casting, or flyfishing, either from boats or while wading. Best baits, lures, and flies include live or very fresh crabs, shrimp, clams, and strips or pieces of fresh conch, as well as small streamer flies, crab patterns, bonefish jigs, weighted bucktails, and small plugs.

Since the permit has a tough, leathery mouth, it is a good idea to strike hard several times as soon as the fish takes the bait. Half a dozen fast, firm strikes is not too many.

The permit is an exceptionally strong fighter on

Above left: Permit do frequent shallow water and fly fishermen benefit!

Below left: The Atlantic permit is most abundant and biggest off southern Florida.

HOT SPOT

Florida Keys

The IGFA world-record listings for permit are totally dominated by entries from the Florida Keys, particularly Key West, Sugarloaf Key, and Matecumbe Key.

There are several methods for catching permit in the Keys. The fish turn up sporadically while anglers are hunting bonefish, snapper, or tarpon on the flats and along channel edges, or they may be chummed over deeper wrecks and isolated reef pinnacles and outcrops. But for true permit specialists, the only method is to pole or wade as quietly as possible through the slightly deeper water along the outside edge of the flats and seek these fish in a one-on-one battle of wits.

Permit may turn up at almost any time of the year around the Keys, though the record book suggests March and April are the prime months. Lodges and fishing guides are widely available. For detailed information, contact

Florida Department
of Commerce
Room 505, Collins Building
107 W. Gaines
Tallahassee, Florida
32399-2000

light tackle. When first hooked, it almost always makes an initial long, fast run toward deep water, twisting and turning, while pausing occasionally to bump its head on the bottom or rub its mouth in the sand in an effort to dislodge the hook. If there is a coral outcrop, mangrove root, sea fan, or similar obstacle in the vicinity on which the permit can snag or cut the line, it usually will. To complicate matters, the permit's tough mouth often allows it to simply spit the hook on the first slack line.

Like the pompano, permit are considered to be excellent eating fish, although more and more anglers prefer simply to snap a quick photo and release their prize.

HOT SPOT

The Bahamas

Permit are not as prolific here as in Keys waters, but the western Atlantic islands and cays of the Bahamas nonetheless provide excellent permit fishing.

Although few anglers travel to the Bahamas specifically for permit, this species turns up regular- ly enough to provide an interesting edge to the area's great flats fishing. For information on permit fishing in the Bahamas, contact

Department of Fisheries
Box N, 3028
Nassau, Bahamas

Sailfish

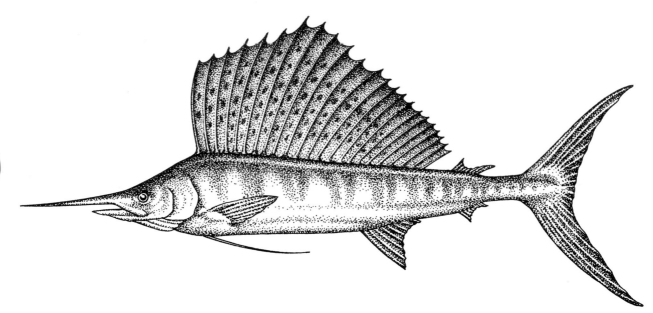

Scientific name: *Istiophorus platypterus*

The spectacular and beautiful sailfish is a favorite of anglers who prize it for its lightning-fast runs, repeated jumps, and strong performance on light and medium tackle, not to mention its striking appearance and dramatic coloration.

While scientists continue to argue about the existence of two or more separate species of sailfish in the tropical and subtropical seas of the world, record-keeping bodies such as the International Game Fish Association have long divided the fish into two distinct groupings, the Atlantic and Indo-Pacific sailfish.

It is highly unlikely anyone could mistake a sailfish, with its enormous, characteristic dorsal fin, for any other creature, including other billfish. Truly gorgeous creatures, sailfish sport metallic blue backs, white bellies, and silvery flanks, often covered with pale, bluish gray vertical bars (more common on

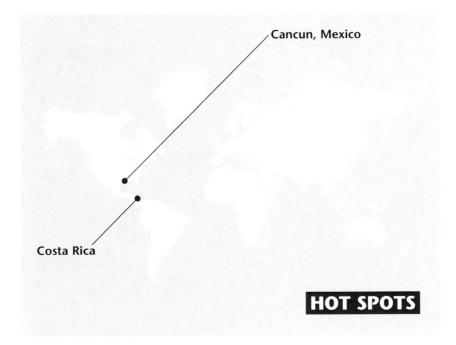

Cancun, Mexico

Costa Rica

HOT SPOTS

Indo-Pacific fish) or rows of bright spots (more common on Atlantic sails). The immense dorsal fin varies from slate gray to brilliant cobalt blue, usually with a scattering of black or electric lavender spots, bars, and dashes. When excited or hooked, sailfish sometimes exhibit a deep golden or bronze sheen over much of the body, which may fade to rust as they tire. This flush of gold is curiously more

common in some populations of Indo-Pacific sailfish than in their Atlantic cousins.

Habitat and Behavior

Sailfish are found in tropical and subtropical waters, mostly near land masses or around islands, atolls, and reefs. They usually swim in waters with depths of six fathoms (35 feet) or more, but occasionally stray into shallower areas. In fact, they are sometimes caught from ocean piers and rock ledges by anglers targeting much smaller and far less acrobatic species.

Pelagic and seasonally migratory, sailfish travel alone, in groups of two or three, or even in small schools of a dozen or more. They appear to feed mostly in mid-water and near the surface, especially along the edges of reefs or in current eddies. Divers have reported sailfish hunting in packs or pods using their sail-like dorsal fins to round up shoals of anchovies, pilchards, and other fish, which they then stun and kill by slashing at them with their rapier-like bills.

The greatest fishing action for sailfish is found wherever numbers of these fish gather and feed on or near the surface, attracted by large congregations of their favored food species, such as squid, small mackerel and tuna, jacks, herring, pilchards, scad, balao, needlefish, flying fish, and mullet. They are even known to prey heavily on toxic toadfish, puffers, and boxfish, apparently becoming slightly intoxicated as a result.

International hot spots for Atlantic sails include the waters off southern and eastern Florida, the Cancun and Cozumel regions of Mexico, the Venezuelan coast, and the west African nations of Senegal, Guinea, Sierra Leone, the Ivory Coast, and Nigeria.

IGFA RECORD

SAILFISH, PACIFIC
Weight: 100.24 kg (221 lbs.)
Place: Santa Cruz Island Ecuador
Date: Feb. 12, 1947
Angler: C. W. Stewart

No matter the weather, giant sailfish can be had.

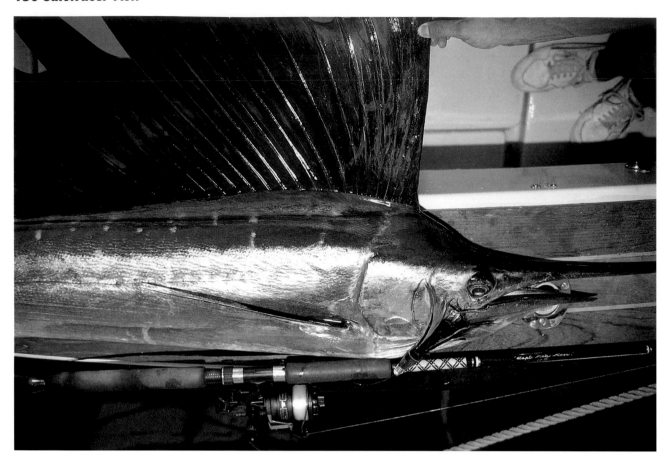

Many sailfish are taken on light tackle, and the fight is always exhilarating.

HOT SPOT

Costa Rica

The west coast of Costa Rica has developed into one of the world's leading sailfish hot spots. Costa Rican ports such as Golfito, Flamingo Bay, and Quepos dominate the record books for Pacific sailfish entries, particularly on light line classes and fly tackle, making this tiny Central American nation a Mecca for saltwater anglers.

In these warm, prolific waters, it is not unusual to enjoy 10 or 20 opportunities at sailfish during a single day's fishing, with as many as five or six fish being fought,

tagged, and released. On truly exceptional days, anglers may land as many as 20 sailfish per day.

Sailfish are available in famous Costa Rican locations such as the Gulf of Papagayo throughout much of the year, although the period from May until August is best. On the other hand, southern ports like Quepos enjoy top action from December to February.

Some fine charter vessels and local sportfishing boats are now available to anglers visiting Costa Rica. A rapidly developing tourism industry means accommodations and full facilities are readily available. For information on Costa Rica's outstanding sailfish, contact

I.M.C.
224 Merton Street
Toronto, Ontario M4S 1A1

Pacific sailfish are particularly prolific on the west coast of Mexico and Central America, especially in the waters of Guatemala, El Salvador, Nicaragua, Costa Rica, Panama, Colombia, and Ecuador. They are also found near South Pacific island chains such as Fiji and Tonga, as well as around the northern half of Australia and New Guinea, through parts of South East Asia, around Sri Lanka, in the Arabian Gulf and Red Sea, and southward along the entire east coast of Africa.

Finding the Heavyweights

The all-tackle world record for Pacific sailfish is a massive 221-pound fish caught off Santa Cruz Island, Ecuador, in 1947. However, several other sails in the 200-pound class have been taken in more recent times from places as widely separated as the Philippines, Tonga, Australia, and Panama. Nearly all the really large Atlantic sailfish recorded have come from west African waters, particularly off Nigeria.

Fishing Techniques

Its outstanding fighting abilities and spectacular aerial performance endear the sailfish to anglers everywhere. While average-sized sailfish tire quite rapidly when hooked on medium or heavy tackle, battles on lines lighter than 20 pounds can last for many hours.

Fishing methods for sailfish include trolling with strip baits, whole mullet or balao, plastic lures, feathers or spoons, as well as drifting live bait and kite fishing from boats while using jacks, mullet, goggle eyes, grunt, and other small baitfish. Sailfish may also be taken on spinning or fly tackle after first being teased to the surface by trolling hookless baits or lures. Pacific sails to 136 pounds have been taken on fly tackle with just a 12-pound-test tippet. Landing any sailfish on fly gear is a genuine accomplishment; landing one in excess of 100 pounds must be considered the catch of a lifetime.

Although they are eaten (often smoked) in some parts of the world, sailfish are regarded by most anglers as a purely sporting species. Most are released alive, with only the occasional one kept as a wall mount. Recent sonic tagging and tracking research suggests that this species is quite hardy, and that survival rates of released specimens taken by anglers is good to excellent.

HOT SPOT

Cancun, Mexico

As well as being an immensely popular holiday destination, beautiful Cancun in eastern Mexico is also a renowned location for tangling with big Atlantic sailfish.

While May, June, and July are perhaps the very best months for catching big Atlantic sailfish at Cancun, fine fishing is also available at other times of the year, with a very professional charter fleet now on hand to cater to visiting anglers. As a major destination for tourists from around the world, Cancun has accommodations and facilities for visiting anglers that are second to none. Finding a good charter boat is simply a matter of visiting the docks at the end of the day when the boats return. A quick chat with returning anglers will point you to the most productive boats.

For further information on fishing in Mexico, contact

Mexican Department
of Fisheries
2550 Fifth Avenue,
Suite 1001
San Diego, California
92103-6622

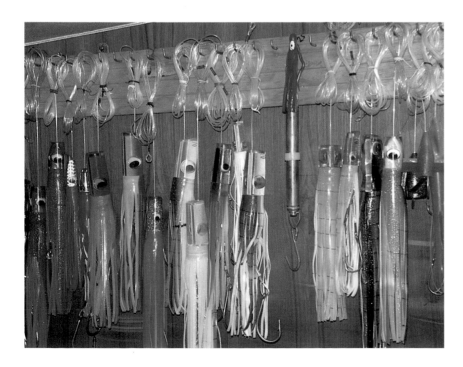

Colored skirts in front of a rigged baitfish, called a "ballyhoo," will entice most sailfish to bite.

Sharks

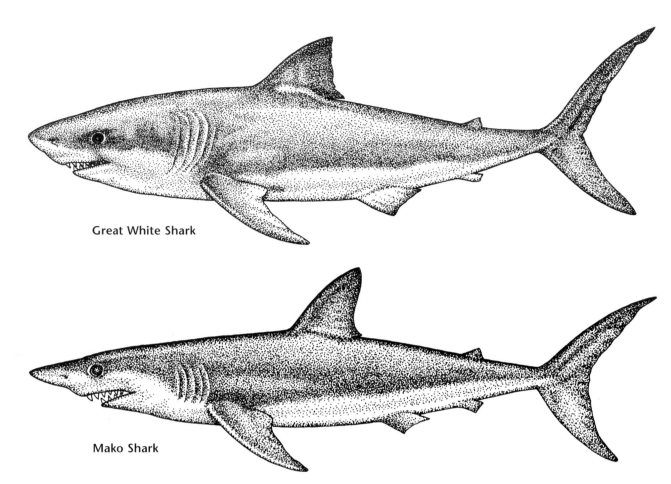

Great White Shark

Mako Shark

Scientific names: *Prionace glauca* (Blue Shark), *Isurus oxyrinchus* (Shortfin Mako), *I. paucus* (Longfin Mako), *Galeocerdo cuvieri* (Tiger Shark), *Carcharodon carcharias* (White Shark)

O f the hundreds of species of shark, only seven are of interest to anglers: the blue, the hammerhead, mako, porbeagle, thresher, tiger, and white. Of these, the four with the widest international distribution and greatest relevance to anglers are the blue, mako, tiger, and white.

The blue shark is easily recognizable by the brilliant blue coloration on its upper body, and its very long pectoral fins, somewhat reminiscent of wings on an aircraft. The shark's back is dark cobalt or indigo, fading to bright blue on the flanks and white or off-white on the belly. Mako sharks are also bright blue, but makos have much pointier snouts and lack the extended pectoral fins of the blue shark. In addition, makos have much larger,

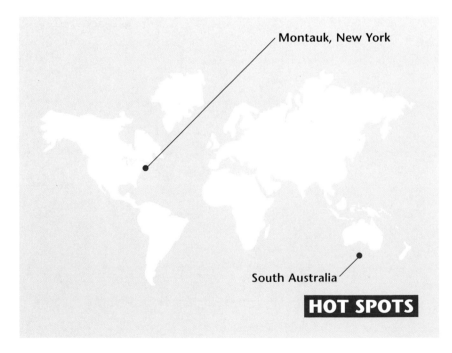

Montauk, New York

South Australia

HOT SPOTS

darker eyes than do blue sharks, and larger gill slits.

The mako shark's muscular body is streamlined and well proportioned. The snout

IGFA RECORD

SHARK, WHITE
Weight: 1,208.38 kg (2,664 lbs.)
Place: Ceduna, S. Australia
Date: April 21, 1959
Angler: Alfred Dean

Tiger sharks are hard-fighting, highly rated gamefish.

is conical and ends in a point, and the shark's eyes are large and black, giving it a cold, seemingly malevolent stare. There are prominent, flattened keels or edges on either side of the tail wrist. The mako ran be easily distinguished from all other sharks by its teeth, which are shaped like inwardly curved daggers, with no cusps at their bases and no serrations along the razor-sharp edges.

The mako's back is usually brilliant cobalt blue when the creature is alive, with lighter silvery blue flanks and a snowy white belly. After death, these colors tend to fade to a uniform slate gray.

Because of its large size, the tiger shark is sometimes confused with the white shark, but in fact, the two species look nothing alike. The tiger shark can be readily identified by way of its

broad, blunt head and its cockscomb-shaped, serrated teeth. Young tiger sharks have prominent, dark brown tiger stripes and leopard spots on the upper body and tail, but larger adults may be much less distinctly marked. Often, big tigers are dirty brown, gray, or dusky orange-red on the back, and off-white or cream below.

The great white shark resembles its close relative, the mako. Like the mako, the white's eyes are large and coal black. Its pointed, conical snout gives it the nick-name "white pointer." However, the white shark is never as blue as the mako, tending instead to be gray, slate, or brownish on the back, giving way along

Above: A little chumming, strong hooks, wire line, and meat will help you hook and land the big one. *Left:* This could have been a trophy! *Below:* Shark teeth are razor sharp, and as they fall out, new ones are ready to replace them.

an irregular line on the flanks to a white, off-white, or cream belly. The pectoral fins may have blackish tips, and there is always a black, roughly oval spot or blotch where the rear edge of these pectoral fins joins the shark's body. The best way to separate the white shark from makos and other species is by its teeth, which are large and triangular, like arrowheads, with sharp, serrated edges.

Habitat and Behavior: The Blue Shark

The blue shark is a prolific and widespread species, found in temperate seas around the globe. The only areas where blue sharks are not found are in the hottest tropical waters and the coldest areas of the subarctic and antarctic latitudes.

While blue sharks are often seen on or near the surface, especially in cooler waters, they spend much of their lives swimming at depths of up to 150 fathoms (900 feet) and more, especially in warm temperate and subtropical regions. Their preferred water temperature appears to be from 50°F to 64°F.

Blue sharks are pelagic and migratory, traveling the open ocean both alone and in packs of varying sizes. Blues will occasionally enter shallow areas close to shore, but are much more common in deep, offshore areas.

For obvious reasons, handle all sharks with care.

Now that's a set of jaws.

Blue sharks are opportunistic hunters and scavengers, feeding on fish, squid, sea birds, and other sharks. They're quick to gather around the floating carcasses of any large, dead animals such as whales, dolphins, turtles, seals, or sea lions. Although not considered one of the most dangerous sharks (owing in part to their preference for deep water away from most swimmers), blue sharks have been known to attack humans.

Despite the blue shark's voracious and predatory nature, and its swiftness and agility in the water, it sometimes puts up a less-than-spectacular fight when hooked. For this reason, it is much less popular among anglers than the mako. Their limited sporting qualities also help account for some of the captures of large blue sharks on very light tackle.

Habitat and Behavior: The Mako Shark

There are two almost identical species of mako shark, sometimes known as the shortfin and longfin mako. Mako sharks of one or both types are found throughout the seas of the world, mostly in subtropical and warm temperate seas. These solitary, pelagic, fast-swimming sharks rarely come into shallow water close to shore, which is a very good thing for swimmers. They are like swimming meat processors.

Makos are active hunters, preying on squid, fish, and other sharks, as well as occasionally scavenging on carrion. The mako is a known enemy of the broadbill swordfish. In one reported case, a 730-pound mako shark was found to have swallowed a 120-pound swordfish in a single bite!

An active, alert species, the mako does attack humans and is the undisputed leader in attacks on boats. A hooked mako will sometimes leap as high as 30 feet out of the water, and occasionally these jumping sharks crash down on or into a boat. Even when not hooked, they are known for

HOT SPOT

Montauk, New York

Perhaps the only area to rival Australia for big shark thrills, Montauk has produced numerous IGFA record catches, plus many more fish that for one reason or another never made it to the record book.

Montauk is located on Long Island in New York, just a short ride from some of the North Atlantic's finest deepwater shark fishing. The area is particularly productive for big blue sharks.

Charter boats and accommodations in this area are relatively abundant. Anglers seriously interested in a Montauk shark trip should contact

Montauk Sport Fishing
P.O. Box 5029
Montauk, New York
11954

their habit of charging and biting boats.

Habitat and Behavior: The Tiger Shark

The huge and extremely dangerous tiger shark is found in tropical, sub-tropical, and warm temperate seas around the world, sometimes wandering into cooler waters while traveling in equatorial currents like the Gulf Stream.

This species is especially dangerous to man, and has been connected with numerous fatal attacks around the world, especially in tropical latitudes. Tiger sharks may appear to be sluggish swimmers under normal circumstances, but they become much more active and unpredictable when food or blood is present in the water.

Tigers are famous for eating all manner of strange items, including steel cans, boat cushions, cardboard boxes, and other flotsam and jetsam. However, their main diet consists of stingrays, smaller sharks, fish, aquatic mammals such as seals or dolphins, and carrion.

The tiger shark is a hard-pulling, if unspectacular, fighter that is valued more for its potentially large size than its pound-for-pound performance. Battles with big tigers have been likened to connecting one's line to a slowly moving truck.

Habitat and Behavior: The White Shark

Variously known as the white pointer, great white shark, or even great white death, the white shark was immortalized in *Jaws*, the famous movies of the 1970s.

White sharks are not especially prevalent or prolific anywhere these days, but do occur sporadically worldwide. While most common in cool and temperate waters, they will also enter subtropical areas at times, particularly in winter. The white shark is most abundant in parts of the central and western Pacific and the Southern and Indian oceans, especially around Australia, New Zealand, and South Africa. On the Pacific coast of North America, it stays mainly in the cool, southbound inshore currents along the Californian coast, but is rare in that state's warmer, offshore waters. On the Atlantic seaboard, it is known to occur at least as far north as Nova Scotia in Canada and northern Spain in the eastern Atlantic. During winter, whites range south to Florida, the Gulf of Mexico, and the West Indies, but apparently most migrate north again in the summer. White sharks are also known to enter the Mediterranean Sea.

White sharks inhabit a broad range of habitats, from very deep, offshore waters to shallow, inshore areas, especially around islands and reefs. Their distribution is largely tied to the seasonal abundance of different food sources, such as seals, dolphins, whales, stingrays, squid, smaller sharks, and fish. They will also feed on carrion, sometimes gathering in numbers around a floating whale carcass.

Great white sharks are especially dangerous to humans. They have been involved in numerous fatal attacks on swimmers, divers, and surfers. This species has

Although sluggish in its habits, the sand tiger will enter the shallows for food.

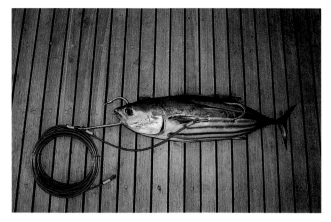

A classic bonito rig for a giant shark.

also been known to attack small boats – sometimes sinking them – and will often bite the propellers, rudders, and outboard legs of even large vessels.

When hooked, the white shark is a powerful and surprisingly fast opponent, sometimes clearing the water completely in its attempt to escape, and often rolling on the wire or cable leader and chafing through the line with its sandpapery skin.

White sharks are thought to be in decline in many areas, and increasingly sport anglers choose to release any whites they hook, marveling at the spectacular encounter with such a fearsome and magnificent predator, without feeling the need to kill it.

Finding the Heavyweights

Although blue sharks reach lengths of 12 feet, they are quite lightly built and do not attain the massive weights of many other sharks. Mako sharks can be very large. Makos in excess of 1,000 pounds have been caught over the years in areas as widely separated as Mauritius, Australia, New Zealand, Hawaii, and New York. A tiger shark of 1,780 pounds was taken off South Carolina. It is likely that even larger tigers, some of which might exceed 2,000 pounds, currently swim somewhere in the world's warm seas. Exceptionally long-lived white sharks are known to reach more than 20 feet in length. Some of these giants may weigh as much as 6,000 pounds.

Fishing Techniques

The primary method for catching sharks involves anchoring or drifting, while chumming with a mixture of chopped and ground fish flesh, fish blood, or tuna oil. Relatively large baits of whole or cut dead fish, rigged on large hooks and attached to heavy wire, cable, or chain leaders, are then presented in the chum trail.

Live baits are also very effective for active sharks, especially makos. These baits may be either drifted or slowly trolled, with or without the added attraction of a chum trail.

Occasionally, sharks will strike at lures and flies. This behavior is more common in warm tropical seas, but may be encouraged in cooler waters by chumming and teasing sharks into a feeding frenzy.

The flesh of most sharks is edible and quite tasty, especially in small to mid-sized specimens. Mako shark meat is held in high regard throughout much of the world. However, all sharks destined for the table should be killed, bled, and cleaned promptly to avoid a build-up of ammonia in the flesh. Very large sharks typically carry heavy concentrations of contaminants and heavy metals, such as mercury. For this reason, frequent meals of big sharks should be avoided.

HOT SPOT

South Australia and New South Wales

Australia is the acknowledged home of some of the finest shark fishing in the world today. All the popular species are available in the continent's warm, clear waters, and the record charts for whites, blues, makos, and tigers are thoroughly dominated by Australian fish.

Two of the very best areas in Australia for shark hunting are the waters off the western half of South Australia, and the more heavily populated stretch of the New South Wales' coastline around Sydney, Australia's largest city.

South Australia is the source of practically all the white sharks over 1,000 pounds caught in Australia today, especially since the closure of the whaling station at Moreton Bay, Queensland, during the 1960s. The peak months for great white sharks in South Australia are November through April, and the most productive ports are Whyalia, Port Lincoln, Ceduna, and Streaky Bay.

Off Sydney, sharks can be caught year-round, particularly blues and makos, with increasing numbers of tigers available during the southern summer months of January, February, March, and April.

Fine charter fleets are available in both areas to cater to visiting sport and game anglers. For information on guides, charter boats, and so on, contact

Angling Adventures
P.O. Box 4094
Geelong, VIC, 3200 Australia

Snook

Scientific name: *Centropomus undecimalis*

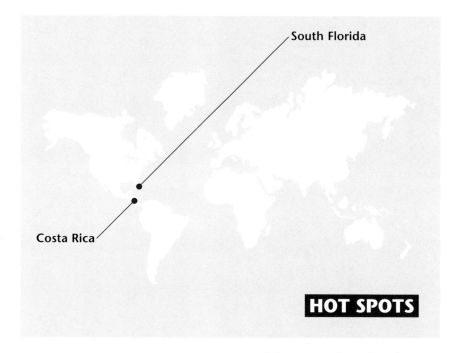

HOT SPOTS

South Florida

Costa Rica

The common snook, or robalo, as it is sometimes known, is an exceptionally popular game-fish found in the warm, inshore and estuarine regions of the western, tropical, and subtropical Atlantic Ocean and Caribbean Sea, ranging from the Gulf of Mexico and Florida in the north to Brazil in the south. On the Pacific coast, snook may be found in the warm, coastal waters of the eastern Pacific, from the Baja California peninsula and the Mexican west coast southward to Peru.

The snook is a very distinctive-looking fish, and would be difficult to confuse with any other species found in the same waters. The lower jaw protrudes pugnaciously beyond the upper, and prominent black lateral lines run from the top of the gill covers back along both flanks to the end of the fish's tail. These lines stand out clearly, giving the fish its handle, "line-sides."

The coloration of the snook varies from place to place, and may even differ among individual specimens taken from the same location. Most adult snook, however, are brown, brown-gold, olive green, or dark gray to black on the upper back, with lighter flanks fading to a silvery white belly. The back is capped with two large fins, the first sharply spined.

Habitat and Behavior

Snook are coastal fish, found inshore under bridges and docks, as well as around the edges of mangrove forests, in lagoons, canals, streams, and estuaries containing salt or brackish water. Occasionally, snook will range inland, traveling well into the freshwater reaches of coastal rivers and marshes. This habitat puts them within easy reach of anglers fishing from small boats or even off shoreline jetties or piers. Their habit of hanging around complex cover, such as mangroves, can make snook particularly difficult to land, and the angler has to match his or her tackle more to the water than to the fish itself.

Snook eat small fish and crustaceans, especially shrimp and crabs, which they hunt around structure. Pinfish in particular make excellent live or dead baits for snook. They're ambush hunters, using a fast lunge and the sudden, vicious extension of their cavernous mouth to secure its hapless prey.

The snook's keen eyes are well adapted to low light conditions. The fish often hunt actively at night, during dawn and dusk, and in the roiled, muddied water of tidal rips and river mouths or bars. During the brightest part of the day, larger snook seek the shelter of overhanging vegetation, bridges, or other cover.

Snook usually mature by their third year of life and are believed to have a life span of at least seven years. They are very sensitive to low water temperatures, and cannot survive in areas where the water drops below about 60°F.

The color of snook varies according to habitat, but all have a pronounced black lateral stripe.

Finding the Heavyweights

Snook occasionally reach weights up to 40 pounds or more, although fish over 20 pounds are considered trophy fish, especially in Florida waters and the Gulf of Mexico. The very largest snook come from Central American destinations, particularly Costa Rica.

Fishing Techniques

Fishermen target snook with a range of spinning, flyfishing, and baitfishing tackle, prizing it for its hard strikes, spectacular jumps, and strong fights. Anglers who enjoy fishing for largemouth bass will find themselves right at

IGFA RECORD

SNOOK, COMMON
Weight: 24.32 kg (53 lbs. 10 oz.)
Place: Parismina Ranch, Costa Rica
Date: Oct. 18, 1978
Angler: Gilbert Ponzi

HOT SPOT

Florida

Snook draw thousands of anglers to Florida waters each winter. The shorelines, docks, canals, and rivers there teem with fish, and out-of-state anglers can find a wealth of accommodations, facilities, and fishing guides. In many places snook can be caught from shoreline jetties, piers, and docks, providing exciting opportunities for anglers without the time for a full day of guided fishing.

A well-developed stretch of eastern Florida between Vero Beach and Palm Beach is renowned for big snook, especially from late April to September. The best spots include Saint Lucie, Fort Pierce, Stuart, O'Quinns Channel, Port Salerno, Jupiter Inlet, and Riviera Beach. The town of Stuart makes a fine base from which to explore the area's excellent angling potential. Numerous record snook have been caught there, and the area offers numerous good skippers and guides.

For detailed information on guides, boat rentals, accommodations, and more, contact

Florida Department
of Commerce
Room 505, Collins Building
107 W. Gaines
Tallahassee, Florida
32399-2000

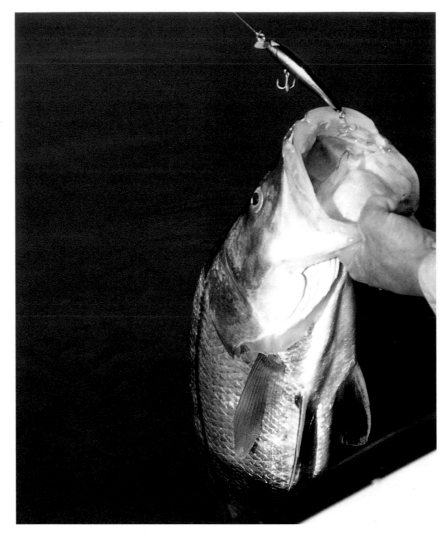

The snook has a large toothless jaw and can be handled quite easily, in a similar fashion to the largemouth bass.

home chasing snook. The fish enthusiastically hit most lures manufactured for largemouth bass, including large weedless jigs, crankbaits, spinnerbaits, and topwater plugs. Many anglers fish for snook with topwater baits exclusively, cherishing the intense surface strikes over all else.

Because snook tend to sit close to or right in heavy cover, pinpoint casting skill is a must. At times they can prove quite frustrating, refusing to move far from the cover to take a bait or lure, forcing the angler to deliver it right on top of the fish.

Flyfishing for snook is rapidly growing in popularity. They hammer both surface and subsurface offerings with great gusto, and put up a royal battle on even heavy saltwater tackle. Their magnificent aerial performance when hooked, combined with the precise casting required to elicit a strike, has made them a real hit with flyfishers around the world. Landing even a smaller snook from heavy cover on the fly is quite an accomplishment.

The best time to fish for snook is at the change of the tide, especially as the high tide turns and begins to ebb out of the mangroves and river mouths. Night fishing from bridges and jetties and in ocean inlets can also be highly productive, particularly around fixed light sources, which attract baitfish.

Snook strike with lightning suddenness, often catching

HOT SPOT

Costa Rica

Parismina Ranch

Although more widely known for its world-class tarpon action, Parismina Ranch fishing lodge, on the Atlantic coast of Costa Rica, also has a well-earned reputation for producing some of the world's largest snook.

Hottest action for big snook at Parismina and other nearby Costa Rican locations tends to take place in September, October, and November, but at least a few fish are caught year-round.

For information on Costa Rican snook fishing, contact

I.M.C.
224 Merton Street
Toronto, Ontario M4S 1A1

the angler completely unaware. Close to cover, they can be almost unstoppable, often severing the line on a mangrove root or shell-encrusted piling, escaping before the angler knows what has happened. If their first, powerful lunge for cover can be redirected, the snook will usually jump spectacularly and continue to fight strongly, even in open water.

Sharp cutting edges on the gill covers and stout spines in the fins should be carefully avoided when handling these active fish. A firm, bass-style jaw grip and supporting hand under the belly is the best way to hold a live snook. It is advisable to consider using a wire leader to prevent cut-offs caused by the line rubbing against the razor-sharp gill plate.

Snook are excellent table fish, with delicate, white, deliciously flaky meat. Despite this fact, increasing numbers of sport anglers release all or most of the snook they catch, particularly in mainland American waters, where habitat destruction and fishing pressures have drastically reduced the snook's numbers.

Large minnow-imitating plugs, twitched just below the water surface, can attract some of the largest fish.

Docks, sea walls, and mangroves are classic snook cover.

Swordfish

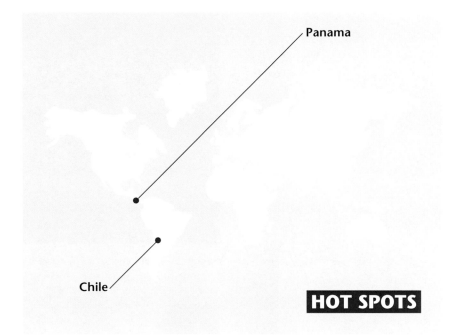

Panama

Chile

HOT SPOTS

Scientific name: *Xiphias gladius*

The swordfish has a smooth, broad, and flattened sword or bill, from which it earns its common name, broadbill. This sword is heavy, strong, and significantly longer and wider than the bills or spears of other billfish. In fact, it may represent as much as a third of the creature's total body length. The swordfish also has a stiff, non-retractable dorsal fin, rigid, sickle-shaped pectoral or side fins, no ventral fins whatsoever, large, dark eyes, and a single, very large keel on either side of the caudal peduncle, or tail wrist, much like the keels found on the mako shark.

The adult swordfish's skin is smooth and scaleless, ranging from dark brown, bronze, metallic purple, gray, or grayish blue on the upper back to dusky bronze or mauve on the flanks and cream to dirty white or light brown on the lower body. While agitated, broadbill swordfish sometimes display irregular blue patches or bars, although they tend to fade to a dull brown, gray, or bronze after death.

Habitat and Behavior

Swordfish are found worldwide in cool, temperate, subtropical, and tropical waters. Mostly, however, they swim in very deep areas far beyond the edge of the Continental Shelf, ranging between the surface layers and the eternal darkness of the great abyss, sometimes as deep as 500 fathoms (3,000 feet) or even more. This love of extremely deep water, their largely nocturnal feeding habits and little-understood migratory patterns combine to make broadbill swordfish a difficult and elusive prize.

Swordfish are capable of diving or ascending through water very quickly with no ill effects, and are also capable of elevating their body temperature above that of the surrounding water. In partic-

IGFA RECORD
SWORDFISH
Weight: 536.15 kg (1,182 lbs.)
Place: Iquique, Chile
Date: May 7, 1953
Angler: L. Marron

1953 WORLD'S RECORD
CAUGHT BY
LOU MARRON
MAY 7TH, 1953
1,182 POUNDS
BROADBILL SWORDFISH
1 HOUR 55 MINUTES - 39 THREAD
LENGTH — 179½ INCHES
GIRTH — 76 INCHES
CAPT. EDWARD WALL
YACHT - FLYING HEART III
IQUIQUE, CHILE

Light offshore gear is all you need.

ular, they employ a unique biological heat-exchanging system to warm the blood supply to their brain when swimming in deep, cold water.

This pelagic, migratory species usually travels alone, especially in its larger sizes. It uses its great sword for defense and to stun or kill prey such as squid, mackerel, reef fish, and various other mid-water and deep-sea pelagic species.

Occasional attacks by swordfish on boats and ships have been authenticated by the discovery of broken swords and fragments of swords embedded deeply in the planking of wooden ships' hulls. In fact, a swordfish once attacked the Woods Hole Oceanographic Institute research submarine *Alvin* while it was operating at a depth of 330 fathoms. The fish wedged its sword so tightly into a seam on the exterior of the sub that it could not be removed until the vessel surfaced.

Finding the Heavyweights

Adult female swordfish can reach immense sizes, occasionally exceeding 13 feet and 1,500 pounds.

While swordfish are found throughout the oceans of the world, they are taken by anglers on a regular basis only in certain locations: Chile, Panama, Venezuela, the east coast of North America between Florida and Nova Scotia, parts of California, Hawaii, and the North Island of New Zealand. Smaller numbers are also taken in South Africa, Australia, Indonesia, and around isolated islands or island groups in the Atlantic, Pacific, and Indian oceans.

Swordfish were once also reasonably common in the Mediterranean Sea, particularly around Sardinia, Sicily, southern Italy, and North Africa, as well as off the Atlantic coasts of Spain and Portugal. Unfortunately their numbers have been greatly depleted in these areas, largely as a result of commercial overharvesting by harpooners and longliners.

Fishing Techniques

There are two major methods for catching broadbill swordfish on rod and reel. The first is to look for cruising or sunning fish on the surface, then troll or cast a live or dead bait immediately ahead of

HOT SPOT

Chile

During the early and mid-1950s, adventurous heavy-tackle anglers pioneered a famous giant broadbill fishery off the deep Pacific coast of Chile, in South America. Fishing off the Chilean port of Iquique, they caught a string of broadbill swordfish over 600 pounds, including one of 1,182 pounds.

Sadly, the 1960s and 1970s saw the almost total demise of recreational swordfishing in Chile. But during the 1980s, enterprising fishing-travel organizers were once again able to offer Chilean swordfishing as one of their more exclusive angling vacation options, and some very large swordfish began to be landed on modern game-fishing tackle off ports such as Algarrobo, near Valparaiso.

Chilean swordfish are often baited on the surface during the day, particularly from March until July, although some fish are available all year. For information on accommodations and charters, contact

Sportfishing Travel Network
937 Centre Road
Waterdown, Ontario L0R 2H0

The offshore waters of Florida and the Bahamas are excellent and hold good numbers of swordfish.

Make sure to change your trolling speed occasionally and that your baits are breaking the surface.

the fish in the hope of provoking a strike. This technique is commonly practiced in Chile and off southern California. However, many days or weeks may pass between swordfish sightings, even at these proven locations, and sunning swordfish are notoriously shy and finicky. Many vanish before a bait can be presented.

A newer and more effective technique involves the presentation of fresh whole squid or live and dead fish baits at varying depths beneath the ocean's surface at night. Often, these deep baits are rigged in conjunction with glowing, chemical light sticks to enhance their appeal. This technique has helped pioneer new swordfish fisheries off Florida, Central America, Hawaii, New Zealand, and Australia. Sadly, overfishing in some of these regions has led to a sudden decline in catches, most notably off Florida, where the recreational fishery boomed and virtually collapsed within a few short years during the 1980s.

As if hooking a swordfish isn't tough enough, landing one is even harder. Swords are extremely hard-fighting fish, capable of sustained runs, powerful dives, and high, graceful leaps; yet their soft mouths and flesh often result in pulled hooks, while their flailing sword can make short work of even the heaviest nylon leaders. It is hardly surprising that the capture of a large broadbill swordfish is considered to be the highest achievement in the angling world.

The swordfish, or broadbill swordfish, is one of the most elusive of all the large gamefish. In some early fishing literature, the name swordfish was applied to all billfish, including marlin and large sailfish, but these days it is reserved solely for *Xiphias gladius,* the Gladiator of the Sea.

HOT SPOT

Panama

Pinas Bay, in the Central American country of Panama, is one of the few places where anglers can realistically hope to catch in a single day a so-called Super Grand Slam of billfish: a sailfish, a white marlin, a blue marlin, and a broadbill swordfish. These four glamorous species have indeed been captured by one angler during a single day on several occasions, although it is almost always the swordfish that proves the most difficult to find and catch.

Swordfishing from Panamanian ports such as Pinas Bay mostly involves drifting with deep and near-surface baits (usually squid) during the night. The swordies here come in a range of sizes, from less than 50 pounds up to 200 pounds and more. Some excellent light tackle captures have been made off Pinas Bay.

The most consistent swordfish action off Pinas Bay occurs during the months of February and March. For information on accommodations and charters, contact

Sportfishing Travel Network
937 Centre Road
Waterdown, Ontario
L0R 2H0

The swordfish who bit this liked the color and had a nice taste.

Tarpon

Scientific name: *Megalops atlanticus*

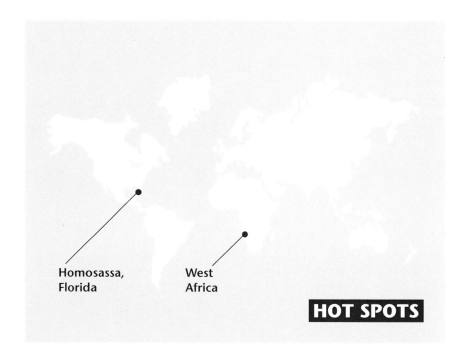

HOT SPOTS

Homosassa,
Florida

West
Africa

In so many ways the tarpon epitomizes what saltwater game-fishing is all about. Here we have a strikingly beautiful fish that grows to the size of an adult human, swims in the warm, shallow waters of tropical and sub-tropical regions, hits with great speed and aggression, then fights long and hard, with repeated, spectacular leaps, interspersed by power-ful, blistering runs and sud-den changes of direction. Yet here is also a species that can be as shy as a mouse, easily spooked by the glint of a rod in the sun or the careless slap of a fly line on the water, and that, on a bad day, can appear as elusive as a ghost. Truly, the tarpon is a piscato-rial paradox.

The tarpon's body is later-ally compressed and covered with very large scales. The lower jaw is undershot, jut-ting outward and upward, and extending well beyond the upper jaw. The teeth are small and fine, and there are hard, bony plates in the

throat. The single dorsal fin contains no stiff spines; instead, it consists entirely of soft rays, the last of which is elongated and lies along the fish's back, stretching toward the massive, deeply forked tail. The fish's eyes are large and dark.

Tarpon vary slightly in color, depending on where they are found, but most are green or greenish blue on the back and bright metallic sil-ver on the flanks and belly. Fish from dark, tannin-

stained lakes and inland rivers may be more golden or even brown on their upper surfaces and silvery gold on the flanks.

Habitat and Behavior

The tarpon is a fish of the warm temperate, subtropical, and tropical waters around the rim of the Atlantic Ocean. It is found from Florida and the Gulf of Mexico in North America, southward throughout

Central America and into parts of South America, as well as on the opposite side of the Atlantic, along the western seaboard of Central Africa. A few stray tarpon have also managed to negotiate the locks and channels of the Panama Canal and are now found in small numbers in the equatorial Pacific waters on either side of the Canal Zone.

This fascinating fish can be found both inshore and offshore. In fact, because it can gulp air directly into its air bladder while rolling on the surface, the tarpon is able to enter brackish and even completely fresh waters, including some that are stagnant and virtually depleted of all oxygen. Not surprisingly, these areas are relatively free of predators, thus offering a convenient refuge for young

fish – the so-called baby tarpon, which run from a pound or two up to perhaps 30 pounds. And, considering the fact that a large female tarpon can produce up to 12 million eggs each year, there are always plenty of these "baby" fish looking for such safe nurseries.

Tarpon eggs hatch at sea and the eel-like larvae gradually drift inshore with the current, where they undergo an amazing transformation, shrinking to half their previous size and taking on the more recognizable features of

the adult fish as they begin to grow once again. Tarpon, bonefish, ladyfish, and eels all undergo a similar juvenile stage, although the first three named all have forked tails, even at the larval state, while eels do not.

Tarpon feed on a broad range of vertebrate and invertebrate creatures, including small fish, shrimp, crabs, and squid. Small tarpon will also take larger planktonic organisms, and may even consume vegetable matter and detritus at times. Adult tarpon feed anywhere between the sur-

IGFA RECORD

TARPON
Weight: 128.50 kg (283 lbs. 4 oz.)
Place: Sherbro Island, Sierra Leone
Date: April 16, 1991
Angler: Yvon Victor Sebag

This 140-pound trophy was taken on a fly in the Florida Everglades.

The tarpon is one of the most prolific of all fish; a single large female may contain more than 12 million eggs.

face and the sea bed, and usually engulf their prey whole, approaching rapidly from beneath and behind, then snapping open their cavernous, bony jaws and flaring their gills to draw in a considerable volume of water, along with the hapless fish or shrimp.

HOT SPOT

Homosassa, Florida

While famous angling destinations in the Florida Keys, such as Marathon and Key West, are justifiably renowned for producing good numbers of middle-sized to large tarpon, record seekers chasing truly exceptional fish often set their sights a little farther north, to the area from Homosassa to Boca Grande.

Homosassa and Homosassa Springs lie on the central western Gulf Coast of Florida, north of Tampa and west of Orlando. Here, myriad islands, flats, and channels provide a happy hunting ground for serious tarpon fishing addicts. While they might enjoy only one or two shots at a fish each day in this region (even fewer at times), these anglers know that there are more silver kings in excess of 150 pounds here than just about anywhere else outside of remote parts of Central America and west Africa.

April and May are the prime months for really big tarpon around Homosassa. Finding a good guide and a place to stay is easy in this attractive area.

CONTACT
Florida Department of Commerce
Room 505, Collins Building
107 W. Gaines
Tallahassee, Florida
32399-2000

Boca Grande Chamber of Commerce
Box 704
Boca Grande, Florida 33921

Finding the Heavyweights

Tarpon grow reasonably slowly, taking six or seven years to reach sexual maturity, at which point they may be as much as four feet in length. At this size, they can range freely into rivers, coastal lakes, brackish estuary waters, and the open ocean, although they rarely travel far from land, preferring to cruise the flats, channels, and holes of the coastal fringe. Tarpon regularly attain lengths of six feet and weights of well over 100 pounds. They have been known to exceed seven feet and 200 pounds, while truly exceptional specimens, particularly from west African waters, top 300 pounds.

Fishing Techniques

Fishing methods for tarpon range from still fishing or drifting with live or dead baits

West Africa

A string of small west African countries with Atlantic seaboards boast the world's largest tarpon. Only rare specimens from isolated lakes and estuaries in South America, like Venezuela's Lake Maracaibo, come anywhere near the size of these west African giants.

Gabon and Sierra Leone in particular can lay claim to having the kind of tarpon most of us can only dream about. Gabon, which lies on the Atlantic coast of Africa and straddles the equator, has been fished by adventurous anglers from around the world for many years, producing a string of tarpon captures in excess of 200 pounds, including a handful of fish over 240 pounds. However, increasing numbers of tarpon specialists are now looking a little farther north and west to the even smaller and more isolated country of Sierra Leone.

The hot spot in Sierra Leone is a giant sheltered estuary system, largely enclosed by Sherbro Island. Here swim enormous tarpon weighing at least 300 pounds.

Fishing in isolated underdeveloped Sierra Leone is still in its early pioneering days, and many trials await the dedicated angler attempting to reach these shores. The coming years are sure to see major improvements in the area's services. For information on guides and accommodations in this remote area, contact

Sportfishing Travel Network
937 Centre Road
Waterdown, Ontario L0R 2H0

The classic tarpon headshake will make an angler's heart pound.

such as mullet, pinfish, crabs, and shrimp, to trolling with rigged baits, spoons, plugs, or various other artificial lures. The epitome of great tarpon angling involves sight-casting to them with light to medium spinning tackle or fly tackle, either on the flats or in deeper holes and channels adjacent to these shallow areas and along the edges of food-rich weed beds.

Some of the best fishing occurs at night, when the tarpon use their large, sensitive eyes to hunt and feed. Most specialist tarpon anglers prefer to stalk their quarry by day, relying on keen senses and pinpoint presentations to draw interest from cruising or rolling fish.

The flesh of the tarpon is edible, although very bony, and does not rate highly as table fare. With the exception of a few specimens kept for wall mounts or record purposes, most tarpon captured by sport and game anglers are released alive after a quick photograph has been snapped.

This Boca Grande beauty was landed on a large jig after a 45-minute fight.

Trevally

Scientific name: *Caranx ignobilis*

Many species of the extensive and diverse jack family are known as trevally in the Pacific and Indian oceans, and as crevalle or crevalle jacks in the Atlantic. Almost all of them are exciting, hard-fighting sportfish and are actively pursued by anglers using a range of tackle and techniques. One particular jack species grows significantly larger than all the others, and can be regarded as a true saltwater gamefish in every sense of the word. That species is the giant trevally of the Indo-Pacific region and its adjacent seas.

The body and head of this powerful fish are broad and laterally compressed. It has a steep, blunt snout, and its jaws are powerful and lined with moderately sized teeth. Few other jacks or trevally have such prominent teeth.

The giant trevally's lateral line is strongly curved toward the front of the fish's body, while the straight portion of this line, just ahead of the

Hawaii

Kimberley Coast, Australia

HOT SPOTS

tail, is covered with well-developed and sharp scutes, or specially modified scales. These can easily cut an angler's hands, so great care should always be taken when grasping trevally around the tail wrist. Wearing gloves largely removes this risk of injury.

The fish's coloration varies considerably, from dark blue or blue-green on the upper back to dusky bronze or copper in some specimens, and

almost black in others. The lower flanks are nearly always bright silver or silvery white, sometimes with a reflective sheen of green, blue, gray, or mother-of-pearl. The giant trevally's belly is silvery white to cream, and the fins vary from dusky gray to yellowish, often with some white or yellow evident on the lower lobe of the tail. A scattering of small black spots is usually present on the back and sides of younger fish,

Giant trevally like this one are easily caught casting into the reef from shore with large jigs and surface plugs.

IGFA RECORD

TREVALLY, GIANT
Weight: 65.99 kg (145 lbs. 8 oz.)
Date: March 28, 1991
Place: Makena, Maui, Hawaii, U.S.A.
Angler: Russell Muri

while larger dark spots and irregular blotches are sometimes seen on the trevally's back and flanks, particularly in larger specimens.

Habitat and Behavior

Giant trevally mostly inhabit shallower inshore waters adjacent to coral and rock reefs in warm coastal areas of the Indian and central Pacific oceans, ranging eastward to the Hawaiian and Marquesas islands. They are particularly common in the waters around Kenya and some other parts of east Africa, as well as in much of Southeast Asia, around the northern half of Australia, throughout New Guinea, Fiji, Tonga, and the other central Pacific island nations, and around the Hawaiian Islands.

Trevally prey mainly on smaller fish, especially mullet, flying fish, balao (ballyhoo), fusiliers, grunts, herring, and the like, as well as on crabs, shrimp, squid, and octopus. They often hunt most actively at night, late in the afternoon, or at first light in the morning.

Finding the Heavyweights

The giant trevally occasionally grows to more than 140 pounds, but it is reasonably common in sizes from 10 to 50 pounds, with specimens of more than 60 pounds turning

Kimberley Coast, Australia

In Australia, giant trevally are often referred to as GTs. In some places Down Under, they are also called turrum, although this title more correctly belongs to a slightly smaller member of the vast trevally clan – the gold-spotted or Embury's trevally.

One of the most productive areas in Australia for anglers interested in catching giant trevally is the northwest corner of the continent – most notably a wild, largely uninhabited portion of western Australia known as the Kimberley Coast. Here, very big GTs are caught on a regular basis from the shore and from boats of all sizes, although many more larger specimens are lost than landed. The expanses of flat, rocky coastline and coral-studded shallows stretching northward between the towns of Exmouth, Broome, and Derby are among the most prolific for trevally.

West Australian trevally rarely top 100 pounds, but are particularly abundant in the 40- to 80-pound range, making this a real haven for those seeking line-class or fly-rod records. Big trevally are caught all year round in Australia's tropical north, although the monsoonal wet season, which runs from December until March and is often punctuated by cyclones, is best avoided.

For information on guides, charter boats and so on, contact

Angling Adventures
P.O. Box 4094
Geelong, VIC, 3200 Australia

Another trevally caught by casting into a reef.

up quite frequently in some locations. Few of the other trevallies or crevalle ever top 25 pounds, although the beautiful bluefin trevally (*C. melampygus*) may occasionally approach this size, particularly around Hawaii and Christmas Island.

While smaller trevally often form moderate-sized schools, large giant trevally are sedentary and solitary in nature. They prefer rocky, wave-affected, or current-washed areas near the shore, around islands, or along the outside edge of reef drop-offs, but will also visit the flats at times in search of a meal.

A trevally that took the bait.

Fishing Techniques

Giant trevally are much prized for the hard fight they always provide. Many trophy trevally escape in shallow water by cutting or chafing the angler's line on reef outcrops, coral ledges, and similar underwater obstructions, while those hooked in deeper, more open areas use their flat-sided bodies to circle and dive, often for lengthy periods.

Productive trevally-fishing methods include surf and rock-ledge casting, as well as casting, drifting, anchoring, or trolling from boats. Best baits and lures include whole, live or cut mullet, herring, balao, anchovies, tuna strips, squid, skirted trolling lures, feather jigs, soft-plastic jigs, minnows, plugs, large spoons, top-water surface plugs or poppers, and saltwater-sized streamer flies.

HOT SPOT
Hawaii

The Hawaiian Islands represent one of the few areas in the world where giant trevally weighing more than 100 pounds are regularly captured by anglers.

Called *ulua* in the native Hawaiian tongue, giant trevally are caught on both the near-shore gamefishing grounds and even closer inshore, around the reefs, headlands, and shallow flats. In fact, some of Hawaii's largest *ulua* are landed by shore-based fishermen using specialized techniques such as slide-lining and kite fishing from the many rocky headlands and peninsulas. These techniques are particularly popular along deeper coastlines, like the south shore of the Big Island, but are also possible in parts of other islands, such as Maui and Kauia.

Ulua can be taken year-round in Hawaiian waters. For information on accommodations and guides, contact

Sportfishing Travel Network
937 Centre Road
Waterdown, Ontario L0R 2H0

Surface chuggers retrieved quickly over coral reefs will produce quality fish too.

Trevally can be taken with baits, jigs, spoons, and feathers trolled at three to six miles per hour.

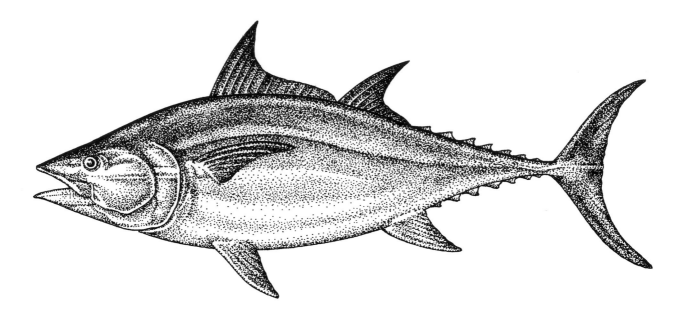

Scientific name: *Thunnus thynnus* (Bluefin Tuna), *T. albacares* (Yellowfin Tuna)

Most members of the fast-swimming, pelagic, and often highly migratory tuna family are of great interest to sportfishermen. Among those currently recognized by the International Game Fish Association are the albacore (*Thunnus alalunga*), bigeye (*T. obesus*), blackfin (*T. atlanticus*), bluefin (*T. thynnus*), southern bluefin (*T. maccoyi*), dogtooth (*Gymnosarda unicolor*), longtail (*T. tonggol*), skipjack (*Katsuwonus pelamis*), yellowfin (*T. albacares*), little tunny (*Euthynnus alletteratus*), and the kawakawa (*E. affinis*).

Of these 11 species, two of the largest and most geographically wide-ranging – and therefore most important to anglers – are the giant Atlantic bluefin tuna and the beautiful, sickle-finned yellowfin, or Allison, tuna.

The bluefin tuna can be distinguished from almost all other tunas by its rather short pectoral or side fins, its high gill-raker count, and the fact that its liver is striated

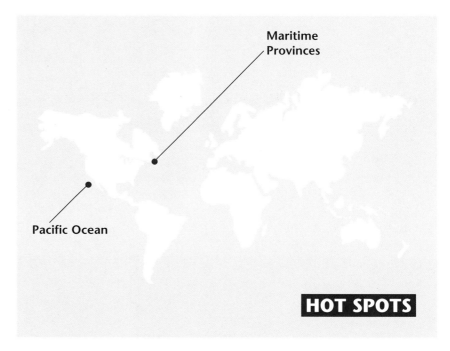

HOT SPOTS

or striped, and that the middle lobe of this internal organ is usually larger than the outer lobes. Its color is fairly uniform, with little significant variation between individuals. The upper back is dark blue, fading to lighter blue on the upper flanks and silvery white on the lower flanks. The belly is white. Most of the fins range from dark, dusky brown or even reddish brown to dirty yellow, although the small finlets ahead of the tail are

bright yellow.

The yellowfin tuna can be recognized, at least in adult sizes, by its overextended, sickle-shaped second dorsal and anal fins. These sometimes curve well over halfway back to the tail in larger specimens, and may even be bent back to touch the tail tips on occasion.

The pectoral (side) fins of adult yellowfin tuna are also quite long, commonly reaching a point level with the base of the second dorsal fin,

IGFA RECORD

TUNA, BLUEFIN
Weight: 679 kg (1,496 lbs.)
Date: Oct. 26, 1979
Place: Aulos Cove, Nova Scotia, Canada
Angler: Ken Fraser

specimens the elongated dorsal and anal fins may be silvery, or edged in white. The small finlets ahead of the tail are always bright, canary yellow and have distinct black edges.

Habitat and Behavior: Bluefin Tuna

Bluefin tuna are found mainly in subtropical and temperate waters of the north and central Pacific Ocean, the north and south Atlantic Ocean, and in the Mediterranean and Black seas. Bluefin are a pelagic, schooling, and highly migratory species. The smallest specimens form the largest schools, while true giants are usually encountered alone or in groups of just two to six fish.

The bluefin's migrations, which are among the most extensive of any fish, appear to be tied closely to water temperature, spawning

but are never as long as those of the albacore.

The yellowfin is the most colorful of the tunas. Its back is a deep blue-black, fading to silver or silvery gold on the lower flanks and belly. A golden yellow or iridescent blue lateral stripe (sometimes both) runs from the eye to the tail, separating the dark upper back from the lighter flanks and belly, although this is not always prominent, especially in dead fish. Light, whitish vertical dashes, bars, and spots may also be evident on the bellies of live yellowfin, especially on the rear half of the body.

All the fins and finlets of the yellowfin tuna, with the exception of the tail, are dusky yellow to bright gold, although in some very large

Big-game fishing gear is a must when tackling the tuna.

HOT SPOT

Pacific Ocean, off California and Mexico

The largest yellowfin tuna are captured on a regular basis by anglers aboard the long-range party boats operating out of San Diego and other southern Californian ports. These big, 100-foot-plus craft range south and west for a week or more at a time, visiting islands and island groups such as Soccorro, San Benedicto, and the Revillagigedos, far off the Pacific coast of Mexico. Here, the long-range charter customers use live and dead bait to attract yel-

lowfin tuna of all sizes, up to and including giants in the 300-pound-plus range. Fish up to 400 pounds and possibly heavier have been hooked and lost in this region.

Some of the best long-range action in these isolated Mexican waters occurs during the December to March quarter, although big tuna appear frequently in almost every month of the year. Fishing from June till October is also excellent.

For information on long-range charter boats in this area, contact

San Diego Chamber
of Commerce
402 W. Broadway, Suite 1000
San Diego, CA
92101

habits, and the seasonal movements of the baitfish on which the tuna feed. Specimens tagged in the Bahamas have been recaptured as far north as Newfoundland and Norway, and as far south as Uruguay. In some cases, these recaptured fish had traveled more than 5,000 miles in just 50 days! The giants of the species make the longest migrations.

According to some reports, a few bluefin tuna can sometimes be found as far north as the waters off northern Siberia, in Russia. However, they generally require a water temperature of at least 50°F for prolonged survival.

The bluefin tuna's diet consists of squid, eels, crustaceans, and large quantities of pelagic schooling fish, such as mackerel, flying fish, herring, whiting, and mullet.

During spawning, which occurs in the spring or summer in warmer latitudes, a giant female may shed 25 million or more eggs. The bluefin grows rapidly, at least in the earlier part of its life, and can weigh as much as 10 pounds in its second year. By age 15, it can be well over seven feet long and weigh in excess of 700 pounds. It is thought that bluefin tuna survive for upward of 25 or 30 years in exceptional instances.

Because of their incredible size, strength, and speed, bluefin tuna are a highly rated gamefish. They are also targeted commercially in many parts of the world. In Japan, the bluefin tuna's red meat is prized more than that of any other tuna, especially late in the season, when it contains a high fat content.

As a result of overfishing

by both the commercial and recreational sectors, bluefin tuna numbers have declined dramatically in the past 50 years, pushing the species to the brink of economic extinction during the 1980s. It is to be hoped that recent wide-ranging international management initiatives have been enacted in time to halt this terrible decline. Anglers can play an important part in the recovery of bluefin stocks by limiting their take of this species, and by lobbying fisheries-management agencies for more control of the commercial harvest.

Habitat and Behavior: Yellowfin Tuna

The yellowfin tuna occurs worldwide in deep, warm temperate, subtropical, and tropical oceanic waters. It is both pelagic and seasonally migratory, but it comes quite close to shore in some areas, and is caught from the ocean rocks and deep water piers in Australia, South Africa, and Hawaii.

Yellowfin tuna were once known widely in gamefishing circles as Allison tuna, although this name has faded from general use over the last few decades. In Hawaii, they carry the attractive Polynesian title of *ahi* (pronounced ah-hee), which translates as "ball of fire."

The yellowfin's diet generally includes flying fish, anchovies, pilchards, herring, mackerel, sauries, and other small fish, as well as squid and crustaceans. It will eat reef fish at times, and also scavenges dead or injured fish dropping from trawler nets or the sorting trays of commercial fishing boats.

The yellowfin is highly esteemed as both a sportfish and as table fare. Its pinkish red flesh is very lightly colored compared to that of most other tunas, with the exception of the albacore, which has completely white meat.

Yellowfin tuna are an extremely valuable commercial fish and hundreds of thousands of tons are taken worldwide annually by longliners, purse seiners, polers, and handline fishermen. Despite this, yellowfin stocks appear to be in better shape than those of the bluefin tuna, largely thanks to the yellowfin's wider distribution and faster growth rates.

Finding the Heavyweights

The bluefin tuna, by far the largest of the tunas, is one of the largest of the true bony fishes. In extreme cases, it can reach lengths in excess of 10 feet and weights of more than 1,400 pounds. The yellowfin is a potentially large fish, often topping 100 pounds, and very occasionally approaching 400 pounds. In other areas, large schools of juveniles in the four- to 60-pound range are most common.

Fishing Techniques

Bluefin, yellowfin, and the other middle- to heavy-weight tunas are mostly targeted by offshore anglers using a variety of fishing methods, including drifting, still-fishing,

or trolling with live or dead baits such as mackerel, herring, mullet, or squid. They are also taken while trolling or casting with artificial lures, such as skirted heads, large spoons, plugs, or feather jigs.

Most tuna, including bluefin and yellowfin, respond well to chum trails. The use of free-lined dead baits can be extremely effective. These techniques work during both the day and the night, although the best tuna fishing often occurs at dawn and dusk.

Large tuna are very hard fighters, capable of long, sustained bursts of incredible speed, interspersed with deep circling and sounding. Fights between anglers and big tuna can last for hours, and have even been known to stretch through the night and into the next day!

HOT SPOT

Maritime Provinces

Giant bluefin tend to arrive in these waters each August or September with the herring and mackerel schools, feeding first off P.E.I., then moving into the Canso Strait area of Nova Scotia during late September and October, before departing quite suddenly to continue their transatlantic migration.

Numerous charterboats in the area cater exclusively to bluefin-tuna anglers, and an international bluefin tournament held each year at North Lake attracts anglers from around the world. For detailed information on accommodations and charter boats, contact

The Canadian Maritime provinces of Nova Scotia, Prince Edward Island, and to a lesser extent New Brunswick and Newfoundland, offer the finest fishing on earth for large Atlantic bluefin tuna. In fact, all the bluefin over 1,000 pounds ever caught on rod and reel have been taken in these waters, mainly from a handful of ports in Nova Scotia and P.E.I. Numerous line class records have also been established over the years at Maritime ports.

Prince Edward Island Department of Tourism
P.O. Box 940
Charlottetown, P.E.I.,
C1A 7M5

Nova Scotia Department of Tourism
P.O. Box 130
Halifax, N.S.
B3J 2M7

Wahoo

Scientific name: *Acanthocybium solanderi*

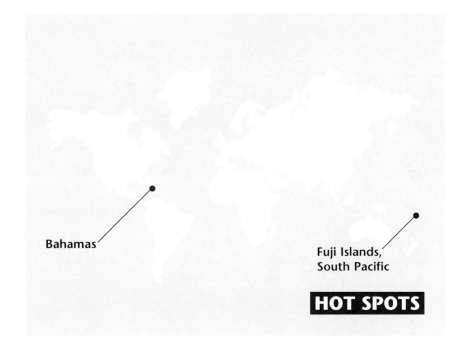

Bahamas

Fuji Islands, South Pacific

HOT SPOTS

Wahoo are a fast-swimming and exciting light- to medium-tackle sportfish that closely resemble the big mackerel species (king and Spanish mackerel) in general appearance, habits, and fighting characteristics. However, wahoo are a completely separate species.

While many anglers target wahoo, many more catch wahoo by accident while fishing for tuna, dolphin, mackerel, marlin, or sailfish. Because of their incredible power, great swiftness, strikingly handsome appearance, and white, tasty flesh, wahoo are usually a very welcome addition to the catch.

The upper jaw of the wahoo is movable, and the teeth are large, strong, and flat in profile. They overlap, rather like the blades of a pair of scissors, and are incredibly effective at slicing through flesh, bone, and fishing lines. The gill structure of the wahoo differs from that of other members of the tuna and mackerel family, most closely resembling the gills of the marlin. There are no gill rakers whatsoever.

The wahoo's well-defined lateral line dips down near the middle of the first dorsal fin, farther forward than on the Pacific Spanish mackerel, and is quite wavy toward the tail. Its back is a brilliant, deep blue, and the sides and belly are bright silver. Vivid electric blue vertical bands or stripes run down the sides of most wahoo, sometimes joining into pairs on the belly. These beautiful stripes are not always prominent in larger specimens and often fade quickly after death to a uniform metallic silver gray.

Habitat and Behavior

Wahoo are found worldwide in tropical and warm temperate seas, generally preferring to follow the Continental

One of the authors lands a big wahoo!

IGFA RECORD
WAHOO
Weight: 70.53 kg (155 lbs. 8 oz.)
Place: San Salvador, Bahamas
Date: April 3, 1990
Angler: William Bourne

Shelf and to feed in waters between 50 and 100 fathoms (300 to 600 feet) around islands, reefs, and larger land masses. They are quite rare in the very deep areas of open ocean.

Wahoo, which are called *ono* in the Polynesian tongue of Hawaii, feed on squid and various pelagic fish, including small mackerel and tuna, flying fish, pilchards, and juvenile dolphin. They are often found around wrecks and reefs, or along weed lines and current breaks, where smaller fish of this type are most abundant.

The wahoo is believed to be one of the fastest-swimming fish in the sea, rivaling other renowned sprinters such as the sailfish. Although swimming rates of fish are obviously difficult to measure in the wild, wahoo possibly attain speeds of 50 miles per hour and more over distances of 100 yards or so. Wahoo use these sudden bursts of speed to attack their prey, often slicing off their victim's tail or rear half, then turning back to consume the remainder of the fish at a more leisurely pace. When not attacking, wahoo will drift along the surface layers of the sea at a sedate pace, using their barred coloration and thin body profile to hide in the refracted light and dancing wave patterns until they are close enough to launch another lightning raid.

Finding the Heavyweights

Pelagic and seasonally migratory, the wahoo tends to be a loner, or travels in groups of two to eight fish.

There are, however, seasonal concentrations of wahoo off the Pacific coasts of Panama, Costa Rica, and Baja California in the summer, off Grand Cayman and the Bahamas in the Atlantic during the winter and spring, and off the western Bahamas and Bermuda in the spring and fall.

Most wahoo taken by anglers weigh between 15 and 60 pounds. Smaller specimens are rarely seen, although bigger fish are reasonably common in some parts of the world. The species has a maximum growth potential in excess of seven feet and 150 pounds, although any specimen over 80 pounds is generally regarded as a real trophy.

Fishing Techniques

Fishing methods for wahoo mainly involve trolling with whole, rigged baits of mackerel, mullet, balao (ballyhoo), and squid, as well as with strip baits or artificial lures. Fishing live bait and kite fishing are also productive, but since wahoo are rarely found in concentrations, casting is not often productive. One of the few exceptions to this rule occurs in the fish-rich waters off the Pacific coast of Mexico and the Baja peninsula, where party-boat customers often cast heavy metal jigs or live baits at large schools of wahoo, experiencing repeated multiple hook-ups.

In some areas, the use of wire line is quite common among wahoo anglers.

HOT SPOT

Bahamas

The Bahamas are renowned for big wahoo. The best time is the first half of the year, from January until the end of June, with a particular emphasis on the months of April, May, and early June. Since tourism and big-game fishing are the leading industries in the Bahamas, visiting anglers are treated to operators who cater to every taste and budget.

Cape Santa Maria
Cape Santa Maria on Long Island is a new paradise beach resort and a tropical fishing club all in one. This resort caters to anglers who enjoy a bit of creature comfort. Their boats and equipment are first class and will help you land that trophy wahoo. Bonefish and reef fish are also available.

MEALS
• Full American Plan

EQUIPMENT
• Supplied

SEASON
• Best fishing: December through March

CONTACT
Oak Bay Marine Group
1327 Beach Drive
Victoria, British Columbia
V8S 2N4

Bahamian Department of Fisheries
Box N, 3028
Nassau, Bahamas

Anglers who prefer monofilament or Dacron would be wise to use a very strong wire leader to prevent bite-offs.

Wahoo strike quickly, and usually without any prior warning, sometimes clearing the water completely as they pounce on a lure or bait. The first scorching run of a hooked wahoo may peel off several hundred yards of line in a few seconds, and the heat generated by friction between the drag plates of some lesser-quality reels has been known to produce clouds of acrid smoke, even burning out the drag system entirely on others.

After the first run, a hooked wahoo will often shake its head violently (sometimes throwing the hook free in the process). This may be followed by one or two shorter runs and some arcing back and forth near the surface, although battles with wahoo seldom last as long as those of tuna or trevally of a similar size.

Great care must always be exercised when handling wahoo, as their teeth are among the sharpest of any saltwater species and can inflict serious injuries, even long after the fish has died.

Top: Wahoos are excellent game-fish, usually caught by trolling.

Middle: Bright blue vertical bands or "tiger stripes" flow down the sides on the silver belly.

Bottom: Because of their razor-sharp teeth, steel leaders are a must.

Further Information

For additional sportfishing travel information, contact:

Angler Adventures
P.O. Box 872
Old Lyme, Connecticut
06371

Fishing International Inc.
4010 Montecito Avenue
Santa Rosa, California
95405

Frontiers
P.O. Box 959
100 Logan Road
Wexford, Pennsylvania
15090-0959

Sportfishing Travel Network
937 Centre Road, Dept. 2020
Waterdown, Ontario
L0R 2H0

Index

Photo Credits

Every reasonable effort has been made to trace the ownership of copyright materials contained herein. Information enabling the publisher to rectify any reference or credit in future printings will be welcomed.

p. 25 (bottom right), Atlantic Salmon Federation

p. 31 (bottom), Eugene Hoyano

p. 32 (bottom), Eugene Hoyano

p. 40, Al Raychard

p. 41 (bottom), Eugene Hoyano

p. 43 (bottom), Eugene Hoyano

p. 44 (top), Paul Vesci

p. 47 (right), Mark Krupa

p. 49 (middle), Mark Krupa

p. 51 (bottom), Royal Coachman Lodge

p. 53 (top), Royal Coachman Lodge

p. 64 (bottom), Mark Krupa

p. 65 (top), Eugene Hoyano

p. 79 (top), Mark Krupa

p. 79 (bottom), Mark Krupa

p. 81 (top), Mark Krupa

p. 81 (bottom right), Mark Krupa

p. 83 (bottom), Chris Marshall

p. 87 (bottom), Mark Krupa

p. 91 (bottom), Mark Krupa

p. 92 (top), Eugene Hoyano

p. 99 (top), Steven Cook

p. 103 (bottom left), Steven Cook

p. 110 (top left), Steven Cook

p. 111 (top), Steve Starling

p. 118 (bottom), Steve Starling

p. 121 (bottom), Steve Starling

p. 126 (middle), Steve Starling

p. 133 (left), Steve Starling

p. 134 (middle), Steve Starling

p. 135 (top right), Steve Starling

p. 136 (bottom left), Steven Cook

p. 152 (top right), Steve Starling

p. 153 (bottom right), Steve Starling

p. 157 (bottom), Steve Starling

p. 161 (top), Steve Starling

Canadian Sportfishing would like to especially acknowledge the diligent help and resources of the International Game Fish Association. The IGFA has a history of dedication to the recognition of extraordinary accomplishments on the part of individuals in quest of big fish. That, coupled with a devotion to the conservation and preservation of our aquatic resources, has carried IGFA to the forefront of sportsmen's organizations worldwide, and we at Canadian Sportfishing Productions are proud of our association.